CYCLING in DORSET

David Cheetham

Illustrated by the Author

DORSET BOOKS

First published in 1998 by Dorset Books

ISBN 1 871164 40 0

British Library Cataloguing-in-Publication-Data
A CIP data for this book is available from the British Library

Cover photograph: Melbury Osmond, by Julian Comrie, FRPS, ABIPP

DORSET BOOKS
Official Publisher to Dorset County Council

Halsgrove House
Lower Moor Way
Tiverton EX16 6SS
T: 01884 243242
F: 01884 243325
www.halsgrove.com

Printed and bound in Great Britain
by Hillman Printers (Frome) Ltd.

Contents

Introduction

Dorset is a small county with a varied landscape which can be attributed to its unique geological formation. Its major areas of interest include the Blackmoor Vale, Marshwood Vale, the chalk downs, the heathlands, West Dorset and Purbeck. There are no motorways and because many of the roads follow the lines of Roman roads or ancient trackways it is ideal cycling country.

The coastline extends from Poole harbour to the Blue Lias cliffs at Lyme Regis and between these are sandwiched the white cliffs at Swanage, the sandy beach at Weymouth, and the curving line of Chesil Beach. However, it is the chalk landscape and the heathlands which are the most dominant features. The former, approximately 10 miles wide, stretches in a south-westerly direction from the Wiltshire border to Lyme Regis. Deep, narrow valleys, formed by centuries of rain, provide sources of water or 'winterbornes' to a number of Winterborne villages such as the Tarrants, the Piddles or Puddles and the Cernes. In contrast the heathlands are centred around Poole and Wareham and comprise wastelands suited predominantly to bracken and heather. They have a wild beauty which inspired Thomas Hardy's 'Egdon Heath'.

The hill forts, long barrows, tumuli, earthworks, churches and ancient houses which abound in this beautiful county are all reminders of the past. There are remote villages tucked away down quiet lanes or hidden in valleys which have remained unchanged over time and await the inquisitive traveller.

It is the purpose of these cycle rides to take the rider to each of these regions in order to appreciate the beauty and interest they offer. Each ride begins from a carefully chosen centre and the distance and approximate duration of the journey are given, taking into account the nature of the terrain and the number of places of interest on the route. There are many charming villages and sites of historical significance that invite exploration, and there is something for everyone in this series of rides.

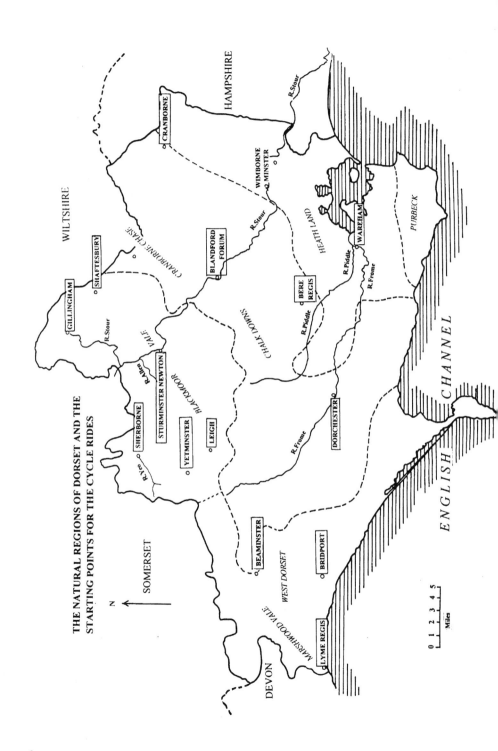

THE NATURAL REGIONS OF DORSET AND THE
STARTING POINTS FOR THE CYCLE RIDES

General Comments and Guidelines

About the routes

The routes reflect the varied terrain within Dorset and are chosen to cater for cycling enthusiasts of a broad range of ability. The rides are between 12.5 and 35 miles long and although the journey time is quoted it does not take into account the time needed to explore the many interesting features which each route offers.

With few exceptions each ride begins from a car park in a main town or village in the area to be ridden. A detailed map is provided for each route, based on one or more of the Ordnance Survey Landranger sheets 183, 184, 193, 194 and 195. The rides are divided into stages, each being described in detail with brief notes on its points of interest. An illustration of one point of interest is included for each ride. The appropriate Ordnance Survey map number(s) and the grid reference for the starting point of the ride, the distance in miles, and a realistic guide to the cycling time are given. In addition, the locaions of telephone boxes on each route are included on the maps.

For a smooth ride in unfamiliar territory, it is advisable to read the route and map carefully before starting out on the journey. Also check the dates of opening and admission times of places open to the public. Waterproof covers for the maps you take with you are recommended.

Guidelines for a day's cycle ride

Your bicycle

For the rides described in this book it is desirable (but not essential) to have a lightweight touring bicycle of the correct size with a wide range of gears, lightweight accessories, a good and comfortable saddle and a strong, waterproof saddle-bag. The bicycle, whatever the type, should be in sound mechanical condition.

Before the journey make sure that the tyres are pumped up to the pressure recommended by the manufacturers and the height of the saddle is correct. Carry one or two spare inner tubes, a puncture repair outfit, a roll of waterproof adhesive tape and a small kit of tools which should include tyre levers, taper-nose pliers, screwdriver, a combination spanner, and Allen keys if appropriate. Check that the bicycle pump is in good working order and make sure that you know how to repair a puncture or replace an inner tube.

If you are returning home late in the evening, particularly in the autumn or winter months, check that the rear reflector is clean, that there is a red rear light and a strong and effective white light in front.

Food and Clothing

Choose clothes that are comfortable and can accommodate any change in the weather. It is essential to keep warm when stopping for a break and advisable to wear bright clothing for safety. Remember, cold weather can lead to cramp.

In wet conditions a lightweight waterproof jacket and trousers will provide adequate protection against the worst weather. Breathable waterproofs are now available.

Don't set out on an empty stomach and be sure to take a water bottle and a small supply of food, which may be selected from fresh fruit, chocolate, fruit cake and/or sandwiches.

Road safety

It is recommended that all cyclists should take note of the safety rules for cyclists in the Highway Code particularly in respect of the wearing of helmets.

To these may be added the following points when travelling on the Dorset routes:

1. Be watchful for farm vehicles and animals when cycling along the quiet lanes.
2. Take extra care when cycling along muddy lanes, whether the road surface is wet or dry.
3. Dismount and walk, if nervous, when descending steep gradients or crossing busy roads.
4. Ride carefully along lanes where the roadside hedges have been trimmed. The thorns or small sharp clippings can puncture tyres very easily.
5. Give way to the motorist in the very narrow lanes.
6. Wear sunglasses or goggles in the summer to provide protection from the sun, dust particles and midges.
7. The public houses that are included on each route act as landmarks and places of refreshment for soft drinks and food. It is emphasized in the Highway Code that a cyclist must not ride under the influence of alcohol.

Summary of the Rides

Ride	Terrain	Distance (miles)	Start	Best Attributes
1	easy	21.5	Gillingham	gently rolling countryside and attractive villages of the Blackmoor Vale
2	moderate	32	Shaftesbury	Gold Hill, rural landscape, picturesque villages
3	moderate	35	Shaftesbury	Cranborne Chase, the Gussage villages, Chettle House
4	easy	12.5	Sherborne	Sandford Orcas, Trent, views across the Dorset/Somerset border
5	easy	24.5	Sherborne	quiet lanes, villages
6	moderate	28	Sherborne	remote lanes, the Caundle villages, Purse Caundle Manor House
7	easy	22	Sturminster Newton	Fontmell Magna, hill forts of Hambledon Hill and Hod Hill, rural landscape
8	moderate	17.5	Sturminster Newton	Fifehead Neville, Mappowder, view from Bulbarrow Hill
9	easy	19	Cranborne	Cranborne, remains of Roman villa, Bokerley Ditch, the landscape of the Chase
10	moderate	18	Yetminster	Yetminster, Melbury Osmond, Corscombe, quiet lanes
11	moderate	25	Yetminster	remote villages, quiet lanes, the Friary of St Francis, wonderful views from Gore Hill
12	moderate	17.5	Leigh	pastoral scenery, hills, Cerne Abbas and Giant
13	easy	18	Blandford Forum (business park)	quiet lanes, historic villages
14	hard	23	Beaminster	journey from Hooke to Toller Porcorum, hill fort on Eggardon Hill, attractive villages
15	moderate	22	Beaminster	farmland, Forde Abbey, Marshwood Vale
16	moderate	23	Wimborne Minster	countryside, villages, Horton Tower, Knowlton church and ancient earthworks

17	easy	21	Wimborne Minster	historic landscape, medieval White Mill Bridge, Badbury Rings, Beech Avenue, Pamphill, Kingston Lacy House, Wimborne Minster
18	moderate	20.5	Bere Regis	hills, Milton Abbas, Melcombe Bingham, scenic views
19	hard	26.5	Bridport	valleys, hills, Kingston Russell House, the swannery at Abbotsbury, coastal views
20	easy	24	Dorchester	quiet lanes, attractive villages, Stinsford church, Woodsford Castle, Clouds Hill
21	hard	24	Dorchester	hills, historical sites, chalk upland scenery, remote villages
22	hard	26	Dorchester	Maiden Castle, Hardy Monument, Waddon House, Weymouth, hills, coastal views, attractive villages
23(a)	hard (long route)	32	Dorchester	valleys, hills, expansive upland views
23(b)	hard (shorter route)	28	Dorchester	as above, but omitting the Piddle villages
24	hard	19	Lyme Regis	solitude of Marshwood Vale, Lambert's Castle, Whitchurch Canonicorum, woodland and hills, coastal views, beach
25	hard (main route)	25	Wareham	heathland, Corfe Castle, Swanage, Worth Matravers church, Purbeck Hills (alternative: steam train ride between Corfe Castle and Swanage)

Ride 1

A ROUND TRIP FROM GILLINGHAM TO STALBRIDGE

Distance: 21.5 miles Journey time: 3–4 hours

Route Description

From Gillingham the route drops down to the River Stour before rising to Kington Magna, which stands on a ridge overlooking the Blackmoor Vale. The ridge is followed to Fifehead Magdalen, from where it falls sharply to the vale and continues across the flat clayland and over the River Stour before rising gently to a low ridge at Stalbridge. The return journey takes the rider down to the vale once more to cross the River Stour again at the King's Mill Bridge before climbing up to the low ridge at Marnhull.

A minor road near Nash Court in Marnhull leads to the B3092 road, which is joined for a short distance on its way to Stour Provost and East Stour. In East Stour the rider leaves the B3092 for a minor road and crosses over the River Stour near Eccliffe before passing under the railway bridge and retracing the route back to Gillingham.

Most of the villages on the ride are on the ridges overlooking the vale, because the heavy clay soil and its poor drainage qualities make it unsuitable for dwellings except in isolated spots.

This is a pleasant ride in gently rolling countryside with splendid views across the Blackmoor Vale and the route is well within the capabilities of the most modest rider.

Start (OS Landranger sheet 183. Grid reference ST806264.)

In Gillingham start from the car park, in the High Street, near the bridge over the Shreen Water. Turn right into the High Street and follow the road as it bears right alongside St Mary's Church and then left to the junction with Le Neuborg Way. Turn left to the traffic lights and then right along Wyke Street and its extension Wyke Road (B3081). Take the first turn on the left along Common Mead Lane. Follow the road through the housing estate to open country, pass under the railway bridge and bear right to Kington Magna.

Points of interest

▲   Gillingham, on the edge of the Blackmoor Vale, reveals little of its long history. King Canute is reputed to have been defeated here in 1016; later it was a Royal Manor and forest of the Plantagenet kings with a hunting lodge.

Stage 1: Gillingham–Kington Magna–Fifehead Magdalen–Stalbridge

---

Thick hedges line the road to Bugley, the nearest point that the River Stour comes to the

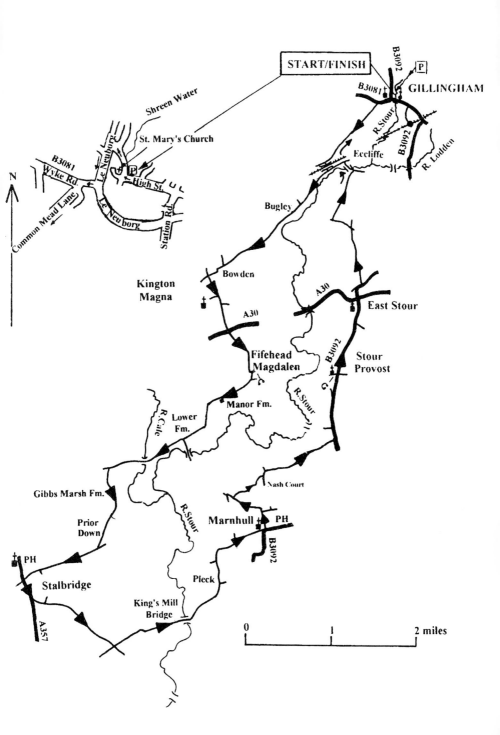

START/FINISH

B3092

P

GILLINGHAM

B3081

R.Stour

B3092

Shreen Water

St. Mary's Church

Eccliffe

R. Lodden

Le Neuborg

B3081

Wyke Rd.

P

High St.

N

Common Mead Lane

Le Neu borg

Station Rd.

Bugley

Kington Magna

Bowden

A30

East Stour

A30

Fifehead Magdalen

B3092

Stour Provost

R.Stour

Manor Fm.

R.Cale

Lower Fm.

Nash Court

Gibbs Marsh Fm.

R.Stour

Marnhull

PH

B3092

Prior Down

PH

Pleck

Stalbridge

King's Mill Bridge

A357

0   1   2 miles

road as it winds its way across the fields. The road then rises steadily to a Give Way sign at the crossroads just beyond Bowden. Turn left towards Marnhull.

The road by-passes Kington Magna and continues to the junction with the A30. Cross the A30 directly, taking care to check the traffic from the right, which is partly hidden from view until it is almost at the junction.

Cycle on to Fifehead Magdalen, from where there are panoramic views over the Blackmoor Vale. Just beyond the village the road descends steeply to the vale, passing Manor Farm on the left. Ignore the sign to Marnhull and carry straight on to Stalbridge. Cross over the River Cale and turn left at the sign to Stalbridge. Pass the industrial estate on the left and Gibbs Marsh Farm on the right and continue to the centre of Stalbridge along Station Road. At the junction with the High Street (A357) turn left.

Points of interest

▲   Stalbridge: an attractive village with a fourteenth-century yellow hamstone market cross standing 30 feet high on the main street. Robert Boyle, the famous scientist and mathematician, once lived at Stalbridge Park, now demolished apart from the gate piers surmounted by heraldic beasts.

Love Lane, Marnhull

Pass along the High Street in Stalbridge, and at the fork bear left down Ring Street with the Stalbridge Arms Hotel on the right. Continue to the Give Way sign at the crossroads. Turn left to Marnhull.

Cross the River Stour at King's Mill Bridge and keep straight on to the church of St Gregory in Marnhull. Turn left down Church Hill. Disregard the road to the right at the bottom of the hill and continue through the village to the next road on the right, which leads to a road junction near Nash Court. Turn left and then right at the next fork. Follow this road to the B3092, the road to Gillingham. Turn left at the junction and follow the road through Stour Provost to the junction with the A30 in East Stour.

Cross the A30 and continue a short distance to a narrow lane on the left (Witch Lane) near a sports field. Follow the lane as it turns sharp left and then sharp right before it reaches a T-junction near Eccliffe. Turn left to Eccliffe, cross over the River Stour and pass under the railway bridge to rejoin the road to Gillingham. Return to Wyke Road and at the traffic lights turn right along Le Neuborg Way and turn left along Station Road and left again along the High Street to the car park.

Points of interest

▲ Marnhull: a most attractive village situated on a limestone ridge and the birthplace of Tess in Thomas Hardy's *Tess of the d'Urbervilles*. Nash Court was the home of Catherine Parr, who survived Henry VIII. The church has many fifteenth-century features. In addition, there is evidence of Iron Age habitation near by.

Ride 2

A TOUR IN NORTH DORSET

Distance: 32 miles **Journey time:** *approximately 6 hours*

Route Description

The ride begins in the historic town of Shaftesbury with a long downhill run to Motcombe. This provides a splendid start to a journey, which remains close to the Wiltshire border before turning south-west, by-passing Gillingham on the way to Milton on Stour. Bourton is the northernmost point of the journey; from here the rider cycles through the villages on the limestone ridge overlooking the Blackmoor Vale. From Fifehead Magdalen, one of these villages, the route leads down to the flat expanse of the vale and across the River Stour before returning to the ridge at Marnhull. The tour leaves the ridge at Hinton St Mary and wends its way along to Margaret Marsh and Stour Row before making the final ascent to Shaftesbury.

Quiet roads, beautiful rural landscape and attractive villages feature strongly in this ride, and the only climb of any consequence is the one up to Shaftesbury on the return journey.

Start (OS Landranger sheet 183. Grid reference ST865230.)

Turn right at the exit to the public car park in Coppice Street, Shaftesbury. At the junction at the bottom of the street, near the post office, keep straight on up the High Street and follow it through the town to Bleke Street. From Bleke Street turn left down New Road, pass under the A30 and take the first turn on the right to Motcombe.

Stage 1: Motcombe–Milton on Stour–Silton–Bourton

The road to Motcombe drops steeply from the A30 and continues to a fork. Bear right and ride through the main body of the village to a T-junction at Elm Hill. Turn left and follow the road as it makes a sharp right turn before passing over a railway bridge and continuing to a crossroads.

Turn left and cycle to the next crossroads. Turn left and take the next turning on the right to Bowridge. There is a seat near the turning. Carry on up Bowridge Hill and follow the road as it bears sharp left and down to a ford. A footway at the side of the ford ensures a dry crossing.

Turn left at the next T-junction and continue to the junction with the B3095. Turn right along the B3095 and take the first turning on the left. This minor road leads to a T-junction in the main part of Milton on Stour. Turn left here and then take the second turning on the right. Follow this road past Whistley Farm and on through the hamlet of Silton, keeping to the left at the fork, to a T-junction with the B3092. Turn left and

15

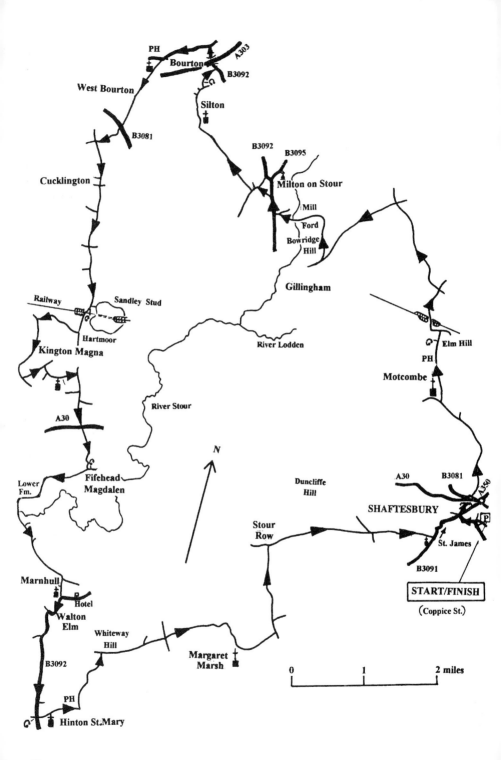

PH

Bourton

West Bourton

A303

B3092

Silton

B3081

B3092   B3095

Cucklington

Milton on Stour

Mill

Ford

Bowridge
Hill

Gillingham

Railway

Sandley Stud

Hartmoor

River Lodden

Elm Hill

Kington Magna

PH

Motcombe

A30

River Stour

N

Fifehead
Magdalen

Lower
Fm.

Duncliffe
Hill

A30   B3081

SHAFTESBURY

Stour
Row

St. James

START/FINISH

(Coppice St.)

B3091

Marnhull

Hotel

Walton
Elm

Whiteway
Hill

B3092

Margaret
Marsh

0   1   2 miles

PH

Hinton St.Mary

proceed under the A303 to another T-junction. Turn left onto the main road through the village of Bourton (formerly part of the A303), then left again at the war memorial, just below the church, towards West Bourton.

Points of interest

▲ Shaftesbury: an ancient hill-top town on the site of a fortress. King Alfred founded the abbey in AD 888 and his daughter, Athelgiva, became its first abbess. It was to this abbey that the body of Edward the Martyr was brought in AD 981 after his murder at Corfe Castle. King Canute was a visitor to the abbey and died there in 1035. Catherine of Aragon visited the town in 1501 while on her way to London. The abbey ruins are still visible at a site near Park Walk. The famous Gold Hill has a medieval cobbled surface with a thirteenth-century wall on one side and sixteenth- and seventeenth-century houses on the other. The Local History Museum is at the top of the hill.

▲ Milton on Stour: a village on the Dorset/Wiltshire border with many attractive cottages. The River Stour is a stream at this point, being only 3 miles from its source at Stourhead.

▲ Silton: a secluded village within a parkland setting. The church stands on a limestone knoll and looks across to the wooded cone of Duncliffe Hill, near Shaftesbury. It dates back to the Norman period but much of the present church is fifteenth-century. In a field near the churchyard is the impressive 'Judge Wyndham's Oak'.

Gold Hill, Shaftesbury

Follow the road from Bourton through West Bourton to the crossroads with the B3081. Go straight across and at the next crossroads turn left towards Cucklington. Ignore the first turning on the right and pass directly across at the next crossroads. Again, disregard the next turn to the right, go straight over the next crossroads and ignore the next turning on the right.

Pass the Sandley Stud and take the next turning on the right at Hartmoor. This leads to Kington Magna. The road falls steeply to a T-junction. Turn left and follow the road as it bears right and then sharp left to the village. Take the first turning on the left and climb to the first turning on the right.

Turn right and follow the road down to a fork. Bear left uphill to the church. From the church continue to a T-junction. Turn right and continue without deviation to a crossroads with the A30.

Go straight across, follow the road through Fifehead Magdalen and take the first turning on the left near Lower Farm. This leads to Marnhull. Follow the road through the village to a fork. Bear right to the church and turn right to Hinton St Mary at the junction with the B3092.

Points of interest
▲ Fifehead Magdalen: a pleasant village standing on a limestone ridge overlooking the River Stour.
▲ Marnhull: an attractive village overlooking the Blackmoor Vale; depicted by Thomas Hardy as the birthplace of his Tess in *Tess of the d'Urbervilles*. Nash Court, the ancient manor of Marnhull, has a history going at least as far back as 1544, when Henry VIII gave it to Catherine Parr.

Follow the B3092 and take the second turning on the left in Hinton St Mary. This minor road leads past an inn into open country, turns sharp left and passes through a wood before reaching a T-junction at Whiteway Hill. Turn right and continue along this road to a crossroads. Go straight across and ride to Margaret Marsh. Pass through this hamlet and turn left at the next T-junction. Continue on to Stour Row.

At the T-junction in Stour Row turn right towards Shaftesbury. Ride straight ahead at the crossroads and start the climb up Foyle Hill to the junction with the B3091. Turn left onto the B3091 and climb the steep St James Hill to the outskirts of Shaftesbury. Continue along Bimport, past a church on the right, to a T-junction opposite a car park. Turn right along High Street and return to the car park in Coppice Street.

Ride 3

CRANBORNE CHASE AND
THE GUSSAGE VILLAGES

Distance: 35 miles Journey time: 6 hours

Route Description

This ride leaves Shaftesbury and runs down to Melbury Abbas, where it climbs to the chalk ridge above the village. From here the journey continues along quiet, well-surfaced roads to the delightful village of Ashmore before continuing across Cranborne Chase to the villages of New Town and Farnham. The 'winterborne' stream which flows through the Gussage villages is located near Gussage St Andrew and its course is followed through Gussage St Michael to Gussage All Saints. There the tour heads towards Horton. This village is dominated by the Horton Tower, which stands on a ridge overlooking the village.

A turning by the church in Horton takes the rider to Uppington, and a short and rewarding diversion can then be made to the thirteenth-century church in Chalbury. After Uppington, the route passes through Hinton Martell to the B3078 and Witchampton. The ride from Witchampton goes through the charming villages of Manswood, Long Critchel and Chettle, which nestle in a rich and varied agricultural landscape. The road leading back to Ashmore, Melbury Abbas and Shaftesbury is rejoined at New Town.

The only hills of note on this route are those from Melbury Abbas to the chalk ridge and from Melbury Abbas to Shaftesbury, the latter being the easier of the two. The remainder of the journey is through a gently undulating landscape, made for cycling.

Start (OS Landranger sheets 183, 184 and 195. Grid reference ST 865230.)

Leave the car park off Coppice Street in Shaftesbury, turn left and ride down Coppice Street to the junction with Christys Lane. Turn right and continue down Christys Lane to the roundabout near the Royal Chase Hotel. Bear left at the roundabout to join the Salisbury Road (A30) and take the first turn on the right down Higher Blandford Road (B3081).

Follow the road as it runs downhill, disregard the turn to Cann Common, and continue down to Melbury Abbas, taking due care at the sharp left-hand bend at the bottom of the hill. The road then bears right uphill past the church, which stands on the right and above the road. Continue along the road as it bears right through the village before rising steeply. At the the top take the first left turn, which runs alongside an airfield and across Ashmore Down. Pass Hatts Barn on the right and continue along this fairly level and well-surfaced road before taking the first turning on the right to the village of Ashmore.

This road runs in a straight line to a T-junction. Turn right, passing a signposted road to Farnham on the left on the outskirts of the village of Ashmore. Continue into the centre of the village.

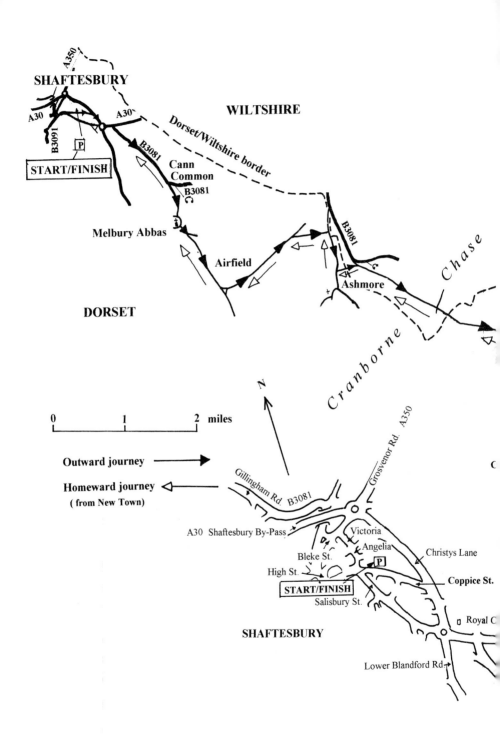

SHAFTESBURY

A350

A30

B3091

A30

WILTSHIRE

Dorset/Wiltshire border

P

START/FINISH

B3081

Cann Common

B3081

Melbury Abbas

B3081

Airfield

Ashmore

Chase

DORSET

Cranborne

N

0   1   2 miles

Outward journey ⟶

Homeward journey ◁
(from New Town)

Gillingham Rd. B3081

Grosvenor Rd. A350

C

A30 Shaftesbury By-Pass

Victoria

Angelia

Christys Lane

Bleke St.

P

High St.

Coppice St.

START/FINISH

Salisbury St.

Royal C

SHAFTESBURY

Lower Blandford Rd.

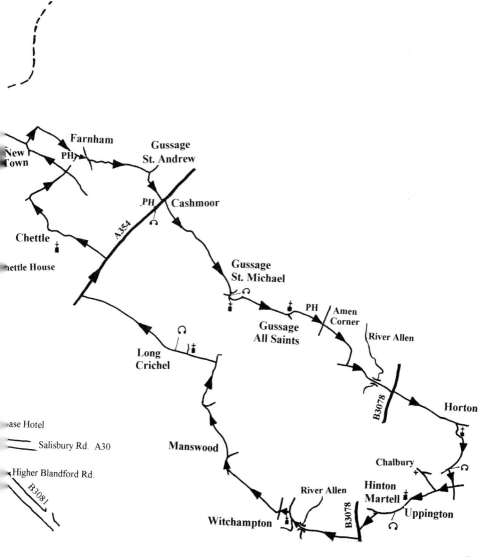

Points of interest

▲ Shaftesbury: an ancient hill-top town with a history dating from Saxon times. King Alfred founded an abbey there in AD 888 with his daughter, Athelgiva, as abbess. It was one of the richest abbeys in the country until the Dissolution of the Monasteries. In AD 981 the body of Edward the Martyr was brought to the abbey from Wareham for reinterment and his shrine became a centre of pilgrimage. King Canute died there in 1035 and Catherine of Aragon visited the town in 1501 while on her way to London. The abbey ruins are still visible near Park Walk. The famous Gold Hill has a medieval cobbled surface with a thirteenth-century wall on one side and sixteenth- and seventeenth-century houses on the other. The Local History Museum is at the top of the hill.

▲ Ashmore: the highest village in Dorset, it stands on a Romano–British site. It is a most picturesque village, with handsome thatched cottages around its duckpond (which never dries up). A Roman road from Badbury Rings to Bath passes through part of the parish.

Stage 1: Ashmore–Newtown–Farnham–Gussage St Michael–Gussage All Saints–Horton

---

Retrace your route to the turning signposted to Farnham (4 miles), which is the first turning on the right. Follow this narrow road and turn right at the Give Way sign. The road runs gently down to New Town. Pass through this small and attractive hamlet and at the fork turn left to Farnham.

Ride straight ahead, past the Museum Hotel in Farnham, towards Minchington. Disregard the road to Chettle on the right. At the next T-junction turn right by Minchington Farm and then, almost immediately, first left. Within a short distance this little-used road bears sharp right, crosses a bridge over a stream and then turns sharp left before continuing to a fork. Turn right towards Cashmoor.

Next, turn left at the junction with the A354 and then almost immediately right to Gussage St Michael and Gussage All Saints. The road runs through these two delightful villages before reaching a crossroads at Amen Corner on the outskirts of Gussage All Saints. Go straight across and follow this narrow lane; it goes down past Bowerswain Farm before rising and bearing right to a T-junction. Turn left, cross the River Allen and ride to a T-junction with the B3078, near the Horton Inn. Turn left and then immediately right to join the road to Horton.

Points of interest

▲ Farnham: an attractive Cranborne Chase village complete with an excellent place for refreshment: the Museum Arms.

▲ Gussage St Michael: the church bells date from 1350.

▲ Gussage All Saints: an old Roman road, Ackling Dyke, runs through part of the parish.

▲ Horton: this village has two interesting buildings: the church of St Wolfrida, a Georgian building built on the site of a priory founded in AD 961, and Horton Tower, an empty red-brick folly built as an observatory in 1700.

Follow the road to Horton and on entering the village take the first turning on the right to Chalbury Common. Pass the church and follow the road as it bears in a right-hand curve before rising to Chalbury Common. Bear left at the fork in Chalbury Common and continue to a crossroads. Turn right towards Hinton Martell. The road rises gently to the village of Uppington.

(Note: A worthwhile diversion can be made by taking the first turning on the right at the entrance to Uppington. This leads to the village of Chalbury. The narrow road passes along an avenue of trees to a grassed triangle of land at the junction of two roads. On a clear day it is possible to see the Isle of Wight from here. By continuing a little further along this road you will reach the village of Chalbury, where there is a thirteenth-century church with a beautiful interior. From the churchyard there are magnificent views over the surrounding landscape. Return to Uppington to continue the journey to Hinton Martell.)

Pass through Uppington and follow the road as it dips down between high banks into Hinton Martell and from there on to a T-junction at the B3078. Turn left onto the B3078 and then take the right turn to Witchampton. Pass across the bridge over the River Allen, bear right to the church and where the road forks, just beyond the church, turn left uphill to a T-junction. Turn left here and then almost immediately right to Manswood and Long Crichel.

The road runs downhill, following a long straight line before bearing to the right. Disregard the turning on the right and carry straight on through the hamlet of Manswood. Continue towards Long Crichel, ignoring the road on the right to More Crichel. Pass through the village of Long Crichel and continue to the junction with the A354.

Turn right onto the A354 and take the first turning on the left to Chettle. Ride through the village and climb to a sharp right-hand bend. Continue to a crossroads and turn left to New Town.

Points of interest

▲   Chalbury: a quiet hamlet which once had an important naval link; a great elm tree here could be seen from the sea and used as a reference point by sailors. The church dates from the thirteenth century and has family box pews. There are panoramic views from the churchyard.

▲   Hinton Martell: there is a large fountain in the centre of this small village; it was unveiled in 1965 by the then Miss World, Ann Sidney of Dorset.

▲   Witchampton: a lovely village with many thatched cottages. An old Roman road from Badbury Rings to Cranborne Chase runs near by. Also of interest are the church, manor house and the ruins of a manorial tithe barn.

▲   Chettle: a charming village, in a location thick with earthworks. Of special interest are two ancient long barrows dating back two thousand years. The village stands in a beautifully wooded area and is dominated by Chettle House, an eighteenth-century

Chettle House

building whose elegance is an example of the Vanbrugh style of architecture. It is open to the public.

Stage 3: New Town–Ashmore–Melbury Abbas–Shaftesbury

Return to Shaftesbury by retracing the original outward journey through Ashmore and Melbury Abbas.

Ride 4

ALONG THE DORSET–SOMERSET BORDER

Distance: 12.5 miles **Journey time:** *approximately 3 hours*

Route Description

A short ride from the car park in Sherborne is sufficient to reach the quietness of a narrow valley whose steep sides are patterned by prominent strip lychnets. The road through the valley rises gently for 1.5 miles to the summit near Ambrose Hill before descending between high, tree-lined banks to Sandford Orcas, a village with houses of character and a church and manor house to match. The manor house is open to the public. From here the journey leaves Dorset briefly to visit the Somerset village of Rimpton. The White Post Inn, an inn unique in having one bar in Somerset and the other in Dorset, is the point where the ride re-enters Dorset and heads for the village of Trent. This beautiful village set in the rolling hills between Yeovil and Sherborne has many points of interest and is worthy of exploration before leaving for Over Compton and its near neighbour Nether Compton. The road from Nether Compton joins the A30 and leaves within a short distance to join a hedge-lined lane that leads to the Bradford Abbas to Sherborne road and a return to Sherborne.

Wending its way along the Dorset–Somerset border, the route offers a relaxing journey with many splendid views over the surrounding countryside, and inspires an appreciation of the beauty of the villages through which it passes.

Start *(OS Landranger sheet 183. Grid reference ST637167.)*

Leave the main car park in Sherborne and turn left into the road called Newland. From there bear right along The Green to the junction with the A30. Turn left down Greenhill and at the bottom of the hill turn right along the B3148. Within a short distance bear right at the fork along a narrow minor road called Coombe Road.

Points of interest

▲   Sherborne: an old and historic town with many interesting buildings. There was an abbey here in Saxon times but the present building dates largely from the fifteenth century. The abbey gatehouse, now the town's museum, is an earlier monastic building. St John's Almshouses are fourteenth century and house an exquisite triptych (*circa* 1475) in their chapel. The Sherborne School for Boys was founded in 1500, the girls' school in the eighteenth century. Old Sherborne Castle, built in the twelfth century, was captured and destroyed by Cromwell. The present Sherborne Castle was built in the sixteenth century by Sir Walter Raleigh. Capability Brown created the gardens and lake which lie between the two castles.

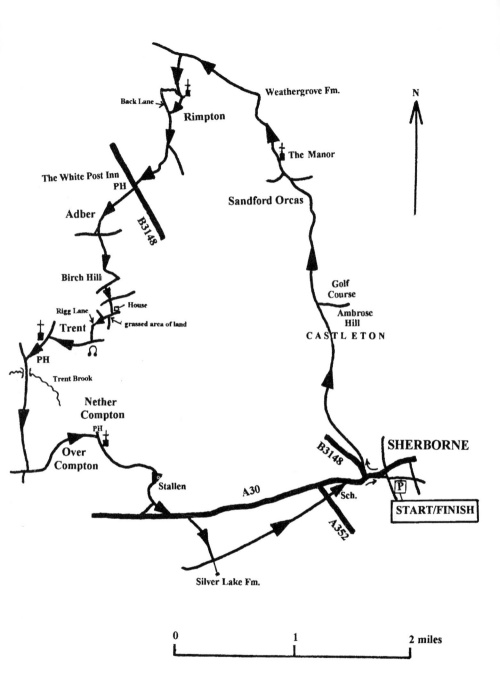

Weathergrove Fm.

Back Lane →

Rimpton

N

The White Post Inn
PH

The Manor

Adber

Sandford Orcas

B3148

Birch Hill

Golf
Course

Rigg Lane

House

Ambrose
Hill

Trent

grassed area of land

CASTLETON

PH

Trent Brook

Nether
Compton

Over
Compton

PH

SHERBORNE

B3148

P

Stallen

A30

Sch.

START/FINISH

A352

Silver Lake Fm.

0   1   2 miles

The road rises gradually for 1.5 miles along a narrow valley, the sides of which bear the clearly defined patterns of strip lynchets. At the summit of the climb carry straight on to Sandford Orcas, disregarding the road to Oborne on the right. The road here is flanked by high banks and conifer trees and away to the right is a golf course. The run down to the village of Sandford Orcas along this narrow winding road is exhilarating but due care has to be taken because of the occasional car. Travel straight through the village to the Manor House and St Nicholas's Church.

From the church continue directly ahead to Rimpton, following the road as it winds its way to the sharp left-hand bend by Weathergrove Farm. Follow the road round this bend and then take the first turning on the left which leads to Rimpton. You are now in Somerset.

Points of interest

▲   Sandford Orcas: a very pleasant village with a fine manor house. The church has some interesting monuments.

The thirteenth-century almshouses of the Hospital of St John, Sherborne

▲ Rimpton: this quiet Somerset village has an attractive manor house and church.

Stage 2: Rimpton–Trent–Over Compton–Nether Compton

Ride into Rimpton along Mill Street, which leads to High Street. Pass Church Lane on the left and carry straight on through the village. At the junction with Back Lane keep bearing left. At the next junction bear right towards Trent. From this stretch of road there are panoramic views over the Somerset landscape, with Glastonbury Tor clearly visible away in the distance. Ride to the crossroads and cross the B3148 to join the minor road which passes the entrance of The White Post Inn. Pass through the small hamlet of Adber and at the crossroads at the small triangle of land go straight across.

Follow this road as it winds its way to Birch Hill, a short steep hill with a sharp right-hand bend. Take the first left turn after the hill and ride to a crossroads. Go straight across. Where the road passes a house bear right with the road to a fork at a small grassed area of land. Bear right and continue along this road, which runs into Rigg Lane in the village of Trent. Ride down to the T-junction. Turn right and ride to a T-junction near the Almshouses. Turn left, pass the church and the Rose and Crown Inn and continue to a T-junction. Turn left, cross the bridge over the Trent Brook and ride up to Over Compton.

At the crossroads in Over Compton turn left to Nether Compton. Turn right at the T-junction in Nether Compton. Pass the church and ride to Stallen and the junction with the A30 road. Turn left to join this road and take the first turn on the right. As this is a busy dual carriageway it is advisable to ride to the point opposite the turning, dismount and walk across the A30 to the minor road.

Follow this minor road to a T-junction. Here, turn left towards Sherborne. Cross the A352, pass Sherborne Girls' School and at the next junction join the A30. Follow the road up to The Green and return to the car park.

Points of interest
▲ Trent: a charming village with several historic buildings, among them Trent Manor, where Charles II hid *en route* to France. A previous Archbishop of Canterbury, Lord Fisher of Lambeth, retired to live in the village and is buried in the churchyard. His ecclesiastical robes are on display in the church.

▲ Over and Nether Compton: two attractive villages, both with medieval churches. There is a sixteenth-century manor house at Over Compton.

Ride 5

THE LESSER-KNOWN VILLAGES BETWEEN SHERBORNE AND MILBORNE PORT

Distance: 24.5 miles **Journey time:** *approximately 4 hours*

Route Description

In contrast to Sherborne, with its rich history, many of the villages through which this ride passes are unknown to tourists. They retain the traditions of generations and are an important element in the beautiful landscape in this border area of Dorset and Somerset.

From Sherborne the route passes through the gently rolling landscape of fields and woodlands in this part of the Blackmoor Vale to the more open and higher land at Oborne. Milborne Port offers a brief excursion into Somerset and an interesting route to Oborne and Sherborne.

The steepest of the few hills that are encountered is the one which passes the Grange Restaurant in Oborne. However, this is compensated for by the long run downhill into Sherborne from the golf club. This is a ride for riders of all abilities.

Start (OS Landranger sheets 183 and 194. Grid reference for sheet 183: ST637167.)
Leave Sherborne from the higher car park of the two which straddle the road called Newland. Turn right along Newland and then left down Cheap Street, the main street of the town. Continue straight ahead along South Street towards the railway station. At the fork bear left, cross the railway crossing and continue to a T-junction. Turn right onto New Road and ride to the junction with the A352.

Points of interest

▲   Sherborne: an old and historic town with many interesting buildings. There was an abbey here in Saxon times but the present building dates largely from the fifteenth century. The abbey gatehouse, now the town's museum, is an earlier monastic building. St John's Almshouses are fourteenth century and house an exquisite triptych (*circa* 1475) in their chapel. The Sherborne School for Boys was founded in 1500, the girls' school in the eighteenth century. Old Sherborne Castle, built in the twelfth century, was captured and destroyed by Cromwell. The present Sherborne Castle was built in the sixteenth century by Sir Walter Raleigh. Capability Brown created the gardens and lake which lie between the two castles.

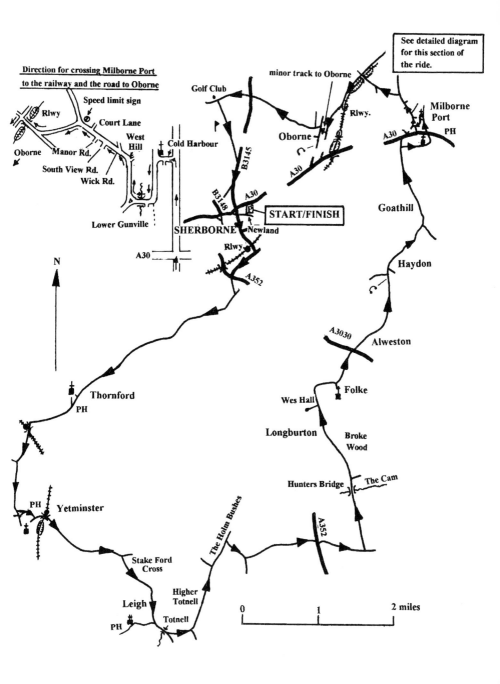

Stage 1: *Sherborne–Thornford–Yetminster–Leigh–Folke–Alweston–Haydon*

Taking due care, go straight across the A352 to join the road opposite to Thornford. Follow the road to Thornford, pass through the village and take the first left turn beyond the outskirts. Cross the railway bridge and ride to Yetminster. Take the first turning on the left, pass along the main road through the village and bear left at the junction with Church Street. Pass by the railway station, cross the railway bridge and bear right up the hill.

The road levels out before leaving the village and then drops down to a fork at Stake Ford Cross. Bear right and follow the road to the village of Leigh. Pass the village cross and carry straight on down the hill, cross the river bridge and climb the hill at Totnell. Turn left towards Longburton at the T-junction, at the top of the hill.

Ride along this road and take the first turning on the right towards Holnest. Follow the road to the junction with the A352. Turn right onto the A352 and then almost immediately left towards Boys Hill and Holwell. Pass Ryelands Farm and and continue to the first turning on the left opposite a Flood Warning sign. Follow this road, which runs alongside a wood and crosses a bridge over the River Cam. At the fork bear left, go through Broke Wood and cross another parapeted bridge.

Where the road appears to divide at a point between high banks, carry straight on, towards Folke. There are excellent views of the chalk ridge and Bulbarrow Hill from this stretch of road. Follow the road as it bears into the centre of the attractive hamlet of Folke. Continue along this road and head towards the A3030 at Alweston and from there to Haydon.

Points of interest

▲ Yetminster: a delightful village with many beautiful hamstone houses and cottages. A number of these are in Church Street, next to the church, which was first consecrated in 1310. Just beyond the church is an old farmhouse called Upbury that once belonged to Benjamin Jesty (1736–1816), a farmer who achieved fame for pioneering vaccination against smallpox. The Boyle's School (1711–1945) was endowed by Robert Boyle FRS (1627–1691), the famous scientist, for 20 poor boys of Yetminster, Leigh and Chetnole.

▲ Leigh: a quiet village with many attractive old cottages and hamstone houses. It has three stone crosses and in a field south of the village there are the traces of a medieval ground maze called a 'mizmaze'.

Stage 2: *Haydon–Goathurst–Milborne Port–Oborne–Sherborne*

Pass through Haydon, bearing right with the road as it passes the gates at the entrance to Sherborne Park. There follows a steep, winding run down towards Goathill. Bear left to Goathill at the next junction. Ven House, the large red-brick house in Milborne Port, can be seen across the fields approximately 1 mile beyond Goathill.

Turn right into Goldings Lane, on the outskirts of Milborne Port, and follow it as it runs downhill before bearing left and then uphill to the main road (A30). Cross and continue straight ahead.

The village cross at Leigh

The following directions will take you across Milborne Port to the railway and the road to Oborne:

Turn left just after the Milborne Port Primary School, along a road called Cold Harbour. Pass the church and bear left along the one-way system. The road drops steeply to a sharp right-hand bend (near a footpath) and from there to a junction at Lower Gunville. Go straight ahead, cross the river bridge and bear right almost immediately along Paddock Walk at the triangle of land.

Ride straight ahead and bear left with the road as it passes a road on the right and the sign 'West Hill'. Carry on and at the fork keep to the left up Wick Road. Pass Southview Road and Manor Road on the left and then Court Lane on the right. Keep straight on and turn left just beyond the 30 mph speed-limit sign. The road rises, flattens out and then drops to a T-junction. Turn right onto this road and descend to and go across a railway bridge. Turn left at the far side of the bridge and follow the road alongside the railway.

The road rises as it approaches a second railway bridge, swings right under a hillside and climbs once more. Follow the road to a partially tarmacked farm track on the right which leads directly into Oborne. Although it has a poor surface, it is passable and avoids the hazards of the busy A30. The track leads down to the main road through the village.

Turn right onto this road, cross the bridge and follow the sign to the Grange restaurant. Keep to the left at the fork on the far side of the bridge. Pass the restaurant, climb the hill and ride to the Give Way sign at the junction with the B3145. Go straight across and cycle towards the golf course. Turn left down a narrow lane between the car park and the golf club. This leads to a junction with the B3145. Turn right onto this road and ride down to the traffic lights at the junction with the A30. Turn right onto the A30 and then immediately left down Higher Cheap Street, to a Give Way sign. Turn left into Newland and the car park.

Points of interest

▲ Milborne Port: 'port' is an old Saxon word for 'market' and Milborne means 'mill on the stream'. This was once a prosperous town with many working mills.

▲ Oborne: a charming village with the River Yeo running through it. It has a long history going back to papal bulls in 1145 in connection with Sherborne. The monks built a church there in 1533, only the chancel of which remains.

Ride 6

THE BLACKMOOR VALE AND THE CAUNDLE VILLAGES

Distance: 28 miles **Journey time:** *approximately 4 hours*

Route Description

The ride begins in Sherborne and joins the relatively busy A352 Sherborne–Dorchester road for a short distance before following the A3030 to North Wootton. From here the route meanders through the quiet lanes and tranquil villages and hamlets of the Blackmoor Vale, which is gently undulating. The pastoral landscape, rich in history and folklore, changes with each stage of the ride. Apart from the gradual climb along the A352 from Sherborne to the junction with the A3030, the demands of the tour are modest and it is ideal for cyclists of different interests and cycling abilities. This is a tour for the inquisitive. It is recommended that riders take food and drink with them.

Start *(OS Landranger sheets 183 and 194. Grid reference for sheet 183: ST637167.)*

Leave the main car park in Sherborne and join the road called Newland. From there proceed down Cheap Street, the main street of the town, and along its continuation, South Street. This leads to the railway crossing. Cross and at the T-junction turn right along New Road. At the junction with the main Dorchester Road (the A352) turn left and climb the hill to the junction with the A3030. Turn left to North Wootton.

Points of interest

▲ Sherborne: an old and historic town with many interesting buildings. There was an abbey here in Saxon times but the present building dates from the fifteenth century. The abbey gatehouse, now the town's museum, is an earlier monastic building. St John's Almshouses are fourteenth century and house an exquisite triptych (*circa* 1475) in their chapel. The Sherborne School for Boys was founded in 1500, the girls' school in the eighteenth century. Old Sherborne Castle, built in the twelfth century, was captured and destroyed by Cromwell. The present Sherborne Castle was built by Sir Walter Raleigh. Capability Brown created the gardens and lake which lie between the two castles.

Stage 1: Sherborne–North Wootton–Haydon–Purse Caundle–Stourton Caundle–Bishops Caundle

Take the first turning on the left just beyond the North Wootton village name sign. This unsignposted minor road, just below North Wootton Farm, leads to Haydon, following an S-bend through a small hamlet before heading along a little-used road. On the left, in a

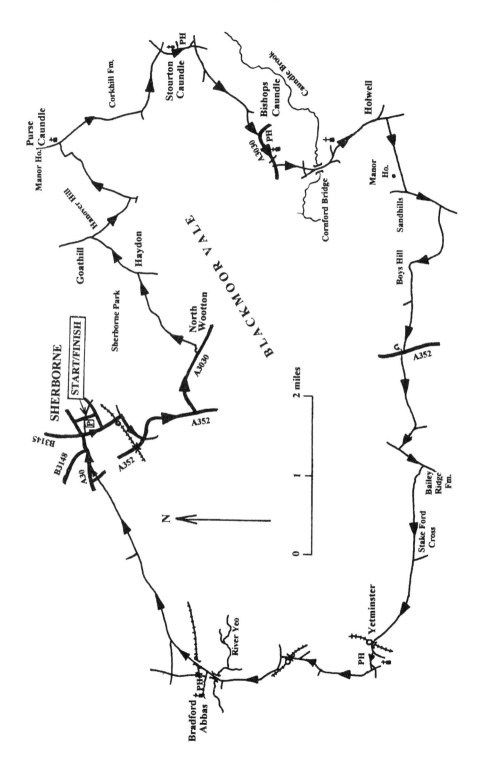

35

field, there are the remains of an old church tower. Turn left at the T-junction in Haydon passing a church on the right and the gates of Sherborne Park on the left. The road winds downhill.

At the next junction, signposted to Stourton Caundle, turn right and climb Hanover Hill. At the next T-junction, turn left to Purse Caundle. Follow the road to a T-junction in the village. Turn left to see the church and Purse Caundle Manor. To continue the journey, return to the T-junction and proceed straight ahead to Stourton Caundle.

The road rises between high banks to a summit near Cockhill Farm before descending to a crossroads. Turn right into Stourton Caundle. Pass the Trooper Inn on the left and at the fork bear right. This leads to another junction. Turn right and continue to the junction with the A3030. Turn right into Bishops Caundle. Pass the White Hart Inn and the church and take the second turning on the left to Holwell.

The oriel window, Purse Caundle Manor

Points of interest

▲ Purse Caundle: a village of great age and character. St Peter's Church is mainly fifteenth century, with a sixteenth-century chantry chapel. Worthy of note is the canopied tomb of William Long, who died in 1524, and his wife. One of the stone slabs in the chancel commemorates Dr Nathanial Highmore (1613–1685), a rector's son from Purse Caundle. He was an eminent physician and anatomist who discovered 'the antrum of Highmore', an air pocket in the cheekbone. The present Purse Caundle Manor House dates from the fifteenth and sixteenth centuries and was built on the site of a previous manor. In the Great Chamber the oriel window which projects over the lane next to the house dates from 1480. The house is open to the public.

▲ Stourton Caundle: a charming village whose church is mainly fifteenth century. The church contains an early sixteenth-century effigy of a member of the Stourton family.

Stage 2: Bishops Caundle–Holwell–Sandhills–Holnest–Yetminster

Ride straight on at the crossroads and at the next junction bear left across Cornford Bridge. Pass Buckshaw Farm on the right, climb the hill to a fork and bear left to Holwell.

At the fork in Holwell bear right towards Pulham and then, after a short distance, take the first turning on the right to Glanvilles Wootton.

The road runs down an avenue of trees and past a splendid manor house to a T-junction in the hamlet of Sandhills. Turn left towards Glanvilles Wootton and take the next turning on the right to Boys Hill and Holnest. At the junction with the A352 turn right and then, almost immediately, left to Yetminster. Follow the road to a T-junction and turn left and then first right to Yetminster. The road drops down from Bailey Ridge Farm to a junction at Stake Ford Cross. Turn right to Yetminster.

Continue along the road, cross the railway bridge and follow the road as it bears round into the village and on to a fork near a garage. Bear right. At the Give Way sign, turn right and follow the road to a bridge over the railway. Cross the bridge and turn left at the junction to Bradford Abbas.

Points of interest

▲ Yetminster: a delightful village with many beautiful hamstone houses and cottages. A number of these are in Church Street adjacent to the church, first consecrated in 1310. Just beyond the church is an old farmhouse called Upbury which once belonged to Benjamin Jesty (1736–1816), a farmer, who achieved fame as the pioneer in vaccination against smallpox. The Boyle's School (1711–1945) was endowed by Robert Boyle FRS (1627–1691), the famous scientist, for 20 poor boys of Yetminster, Leigh and Chetnole.

Stage 3: Bradford Abbas–Sherborne

Cross the River Yeo and ride up the hill. To visit the village of Bradford Abbas, take the first turning on the left. Then, to continue the journey to Sherborne, return to the point of entry to the village, go across the railway line and on to a junction. Bear right and continue on to Sherborne.

At the junction with the A352, go straight across and proceed past the Sherborne School for Girls to a junction with the A30, the Yeovil–Sherborne road. Turn right down Kitt Hill and continue up Greenhill to The Green. Turn right into the town and return to the car park off Newland.

Ride 7

ACROSS THE 'VALE OF THE LITTLE DAIRIES' TO HAMBLEDON HILL

Distance: 22 miles Journey time: 5 hours

Route Description

Sturminster Newton is the starting point for a ride across the green pastureland of the Blackmoor Vale, Thomas Hardy's 'Vale of the Little Dairies', to the villages which lie at the foot of a chalk ridge. This ridge, approximately 10 miles wide, runs across the county of Dorset in a south-westerly direction from the Wiltshire border to the coast in Devon. From the charming Fontmell Magna, the first of these villages, the route passes by the village of Sutton Waldron and through Shroton (sometimes known as Iwerne Courtney), Child Okeford, Shillingstone and Okeford Fitzpaine, their close proximity being determined by the geology of the area. They were built on a narrow band of dry greensand, a greenish sandstone, which lies at the foot of the chalk ridge and separates the villages from the heavy, sticky clay of the vale. In addition each village has a ready supply of springs and drinking water.

The journey to Child Okeford passes between the mighty hill forts of Hambledon Hill and Hod Hill, to which there is public access. The defensive ramparts on both hills are very impressive, as is the view across the Blackmoor Vale from Hambledon Hill and across the Stour Valley from Hod Hill.

This route is free of steep hills, full of interest, and can be enjoyed by riders of all abilities.

Start (OS Landranger sheets 194 and 183. Grid reference for sheet 194: ST786142.)

Leave from the public car park in Sturminster Newton next to Station Road (B3091) and turn onto the B3091, which heads across the Blackmoor Vale in the direction of Shaftesbury. The road runs downhill before climbing gently to the village of Manston. Follow the road as it turns sharp left, disregarding the road to Child Okeford on the right. The road passes the Plough Inn before bearing right. Ignore the turning on the left to Marnhull and East Stour and take the first turning on the right to West Orchard.

Stage 1: West Orchard–Bedchester–Fontmell Magna–Sutton Waldron–Shroton

Continue along this flat, winding road, ignoring the sign to East Orchard. Keep straight on past Winchells Farm to the fork at West Farm. At this point turn left in the direction of Sutton Waldron and Bedchester. Disregard the first turning on the right to Sutton Waldron and continue straight ahead to the top of Pen Hill. This is a fine vantage point

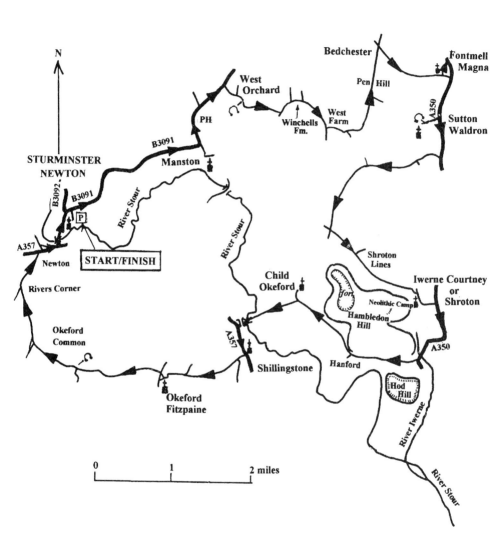

N

Bedchester

Fontmell
Magna

West
Orchard

Pen Hill

West
Farm

A350

Sutton
Waldron

PH.

Winchells
Fm.

B3091

STURMINSTER
NEWTON

Manston

River Stour

B3092.

B3091

River Stour

P

A357

START/FINISH

Newton

Shroton
Lines

Rivers Corner

Child
Okeford

fort

Iwerne Courtney
or
Shroton

Neolithic Camp

Hambledon
Hill

A350

Okeford
Common

A357

Hanford

Shillingstone

Hod
Hill

Okeford
Fitzpaine

River Iwerne

River Stour

0   1   2 miles

39

for viewing the chalk ridge and the villages that lie in the valley. From here the road drops steeply to a Give Way sign at a crossroads in Bedchester.

Turn right at the Give Way sign and follow the road into Fontmell Magna. Turn left where the road divides at a small grassed triangle of land with a 'gossip tree' at its centre. This leads to the entrance to the church and the mill race. Pass Moor's Farm and follow the road round to the junction with the A350. Turn right and climb the hill to the centre of the village. Pass the Crown Inn on the right. The road from the inn is straight and rises to a point below overhead power-lines, then levels out and bears left past a minor road on the right which leads into the village of Sutton Waldron.

For the next stage of the journey, to Shroton and Child Okeford, continue along the A350 and take the next turning on the right. The road is flat and leads towards the base of Hambledon Hill. At the crossroads turn left to Shroton. Pass the farm lane on the left and the area immediately beyond, known as Shroton Lines. The steep sides of Hambledon Hill are to the right. Turn right at the junction in the village, pass the church, then ride to the junction with the A350 and turn right.

Points of interest

▲ Sturminster Newton: an attractive market town in the Blackmoor Vale, the birthplace of the Dorset poet William Barnes and home for two years to Thomas Hardy. The restored seventeenth-century working mill stands near the fifteenth-century bridge and the site of the old castle.

▲ Fontmell Magna: a charming village with the Fontmell Brook flowing through it to the

Defence ditches and strip lynchets on Hambledon Hill, overlooking the Blackmoor Vale

mill, now a pottery. The Fontmell Brook, first recorded in the eighth century, rises at Seven Springs in the grounds of the Springhead Trust. By 1085 it was the source of power for three corn mills and by the nineteenth century it powered a factory which made bottling machinery for the village brewery. The brook runs into the River Stour at Hamoon. The lime tree, known as the 'gossip tree', is a replacement for an older tree around which villagers have met for over 250 years. In the grounds of the church there is the grave of Lt. Philip Salkeld VC, who was killed in the siege of Delhi in 1857.

▲ Hambledon Hill: the summit of this 622-foot-high hill is crowned with huge earthworks of an Iron Age hill fort and the remains of a neolithic causewayed camp can be found near by. During the Civil War, at the time of the upsurge of the neutralist movement, about two thousand of these so-called Clubmen, tired of their farms and towns being overrun by troops, banded together and occupied Hambledon Hill. They were subsequently dispersed by fifty Dragoons of Cromwell's army. It was upon these same slopes that General Wolfe trained his troops for the assault on Quebec. The Shroton Lines was the base camp for the troops.

Stage 2: Shroton–Hod Hill–Child Okeford–Shillingstone–Okeford Fitzpaine–Sturminster Newton

Continue along the A350 and follow it as it bears sharp right on its approach to Stapleton House and crosses the River Iwerne. Turn right after crossing the river. This minor road runs between Hod Hill on the left and Hambledon Hill on the right before passing the entrance to Hanford House School away to the left. The view of the fortifications on the summits of both hills is very impressive at this point.

Ride into the village of Child Okeford and take the first turn on the left (Station Road) to Shillingstone. Cross the River Stour, pass under the railway bridge and bear left to Shillingstone. Ride into the village, passing the Silent Whistle Inn, and up the hill past Croft House School. Take the first turn on the right to Okeford Fitzpaine.

Follow the road into Okeford Fitzpaine, passing the church on the left and bearing right at the fork. This leads to a junction near Ye Olde Bell Stores. Turn right and then first left by the Royal Oak towards Fifehead Neville. Continue to a fork and turn right to Sturminster Newton. Follow the road as it runs downhill to another junction at Rivers' Corner. Turn right and cycle on to the junction with the A357. Turn right here. At the traffic lights at the bridge across the River Stour, turn left, cross the river and follow the B3092 into the town. Bear right along the B3091 to the car park.

Points of interest

▲ Hod Hill: a near neighbour of Hambledon Hill and another major hill fort, its Iron Age ditches and ramparts defend a large plateau. Roman legionaries stormed the fortifications in AD 44 and were so impressed by the defensibility of the site that they built themselves a fort of approximately ten acres in the north-west corner of the plateau. Access to both hilltops is available to the public from the minor road.

▲ Child Okeford: a pleasant village and one of the best places for viewing the chalk hills.

Ride 8

FROM STURMINSTER NEWTON TO HAZELBURY BRYAN AND THE HILLSIDE PARISHES

Distance: 17.5 miles Journey time: 3 hours

Route Description

The ride begins with a steady climb from Sturminster Newton through Newton to a high point overlooking the wide expansive view of North Dorset. This is followed by a rapid descent to the ford and ancient bridge across the River Divelish at Fifehead Neville, a delightful hamlet in an idyllic setting. The route taken through Hazelbury Bryan is along a quiet country lane which passes through Droop to the Church of St Mary and St James, centre of one of the hillside parishes.

From here the ride heads through Wonston to Mappowder and Higher Ansty, where the long climb from Ansty Cross to the summit of Bulbarrow Hill begins. The remains of the fortifications of the ancient Rawlsbury Camp, at the summit of Bulbarrow Hill, stand out quite clearly and there are wonderful views from this high point of the chalk ridge.

The return journey begins with a steep descent to the village of Woolland where the terrain is flat and pleasant for the the final section of the ride to Fifehead St Quintin. The last climb is from Frome St Quintin to the high point overlooking North Dorset. Then there is a long descent through Newton to the A357 and back to Sturminster Newton.

The mileage for this route has been limited to give plenty of time for riders of all abilities to climb the hills and enjoy the scenic beauty and the charming hillside parishes of this part of Dorset.

Special care must be taken on the descent from Bulbarrow Hill to Woolland.

Start (OS Landranger sheet 194. Grid Reference ST786142.)

Leaving the public car park in Sturminster Newton next to Station Road (the B3091), turn right and then left onto the B3091. Ride up to the T-junction and turn left into the town. Pass through The Square and along Bridge Street to the traffic lights at the Town Bridge. Turn right onto the A357, climb the hill, and take the first turning on the left.

Points of interest

▲ Sturminster Newton: an attractive market town in the Blackmoor Vale, the birthplace of the Dorset poet William Barnes and home for two years to Thomas Hardy. The restored seventeenth-century mill stands near the fifteenth-century bridge and the site of the old castle.

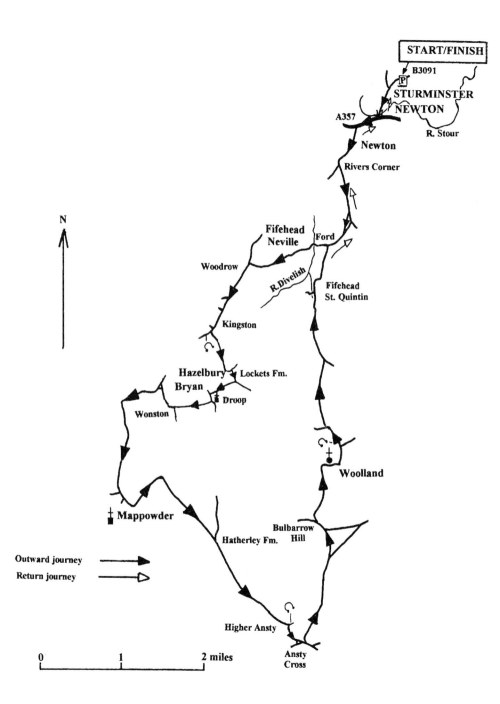

START/FINISH

B3091

STURMINSTER
NEWTON

A357

R. Stour

Newton

Rivers Corner

N

Fifehead
Neville

Ford

Woodrow

R.Divelish

Fifehead
St. Quintin

Kingston

Hazelbury
Bryan

Lockets Fm.

Droop

Wonston

Woolland

Mappowder

Bulbarrow
Hill

Hatherley Fm.

Outward journey

Return journey

Higher Ansty

0   1   2 miles

Ansty
Cross

Follow this road to where it forms an S-bend. Look for a signpost at Rivers' Corner and turn left to Fifehead St Quintin and Okeford Fitzpaine. The road rises, passing Rivers' Corner House to the right, and flattens out near Rudge Hill Farm. Bear right where the road forks and follow the road's steep descent to a sharp left-hand bend. Here, take the turning to the right signposted to Fifehead Neville and Hazelbury Bryan.

This minor road runs down between high hedges to a ford and a medieval packhorse bridge with pointed arches. Cross the River Divelish and pass into and through the village of Fifehead Neville to a T-junction. Turn left and ride through Woodrow towards Hazelbury Bryan. Disregard the turns on the right to Kingston and keep straight on. Pass the point of entry to Hazelbury Bryan and a road to the right called Wheat Close. Just beyond Wheat Close turn left down a narrow lane which runs by a farm on the right. Continue along the lane and through the gates of another farm to where the road winds to a sharp left-hand bend.

Follow the bend and take the first turning on the right. Continue to a signposted junction at Locketts Corner. Turn right and follow the sign to Hazelbury Bryan. The road passes a large attractive house away to the right before arriving at the Church of St Mary and St James. Pass the church and at the T-junction turn left towards Stoke Wake and Milton Abbas. Then, almost immediately, take the first turning on the right. This is a narrow lane with a number of bungalows to the right.

Follow the lane as it swings to the right and then left by an extension to the church cemetery before running downhill to Wonston. Disregard the left turn to Bulbarrow and bear right. Ride through the village, passing the village stores on the right. Take the first turning on the left at a triangle of land near a telephone box. Turn left again after a short distance, at Hill Close, near Clover Cottage.

The road, which leads to Mappowder, drops steeply to a bridge over a river, then winds along the valley before beginning to rise near Dairy House Farm, off to the right. Pass Parsonage Farm to the right and at the next road junction keep left and ride into Mappowder. At the triangle of land with the signpost bear left to Ansty. To visit the church and explore the village, bear right at the signpost, returning to it to continue the journey to Ansty and Bulbarrow.

Points of interest
▲ Fifehead Neville: a delightful village with a mainly fifteenth-century church. In the churchyard is an enormous table tomb to the Brune family. The remains of a Roman villa were found near by and the artefacts discovered there are now in the Dorchester Museum. Also near by is one of the few surviving medieval packhorse bridges. This one crosses the River Divelish.
▲ Hazelbury Bryan: the fourteenth-century church stands high above the village with 400-year-old dwellings alongside; they originally housed the widows and daughters of clergymen. The lectern is made of black oak which came from Hadrian's Bridge at Newcastle-on-Tyne.

The ancient packhorse bridge at Fifehead Neville

▲ Mappowder: Mappowder Court was built in Tudor times and the Coker family lived there until 1745, when a John Spencer bought it. His son was created Earl Spencer in 1765 and it is from this family that Princess Diana was descended. The novelist J.F. Powys lived in a cottage at the entrance to the churchyard.

Stage 2: *Higher Ansty–Ansty Cross–Bulbarrow Hill–Woolland–Fifehead St Quintin–Sturminster Newton*

From Mappowder follow the signposted road to Ansty past a cottage on the right and along the lane called The Green. At the end of this lane there is a sharp left turn towards Ansty. The road runs downhill past the Mappowder Court Fishing Complex on the right before turning sharp right and running along a road flanked by trees and alongside a stream. At the next junction bear right to Higher Ansty. Follow the road as it climbs to a division of roads at a sharp bend in Higher Ansty. Bear right with the bend. The other road, Pleck Lane, is a dead end; there is a public telephone here.

The road from Higher Ansty leads round the bend to a triangle of land at Ansty Cross. The former Primitive Methodist Chapel, dated 1898, now converted to a private dwelling, stands on the triangle. From Ansty Cross climb the hill in the direction of Hilton and Milton Abbas. Take the first turning on the left to Bulbarrow. Follow this road on a long, gradual climb towards a tall steel mast on the summit of the ridge. At the fork bear left, not right as directed by a road sign which indicates an alternative route for motorists.

With the steel tower on the right, the road swings to the left, providing a clear view of the hill-fort earthworks of Rawlsbury Camp on Bulbarrow Hill. Continue left along this road at the junction with a road from the right and turn right down the signposted road to Woolland. This is a very steep hill (16 per cent) and care must be taken all the way down to Woolland.

Pass through Woolland and at the fork outside the village bear left towards Fifehead St Quintin. At the next junction bear right to Sturminster Newton. Disregard the next right turn and continue straight on and through Fifehead St Quintin. Climb the hill out of the village and continue to Rivers' Corner. Turn right at the junction and ride to the junction with the A357, the bridge across the River Stour and the car park in Sturminster Newton.

Points of interest

▲ Woolland: the Saxons built huts here and called the place Wonland, which means 'meadowland'. The church in the village was designed by Sir Gilbert Scott.

Ride 9

CRANBORNE CHASE
AND BOKERLEY DITCH

Distance: 19 miles **Journey time:** *approximately 5 hours*

Route Description

This is an easy ride along quiet lanes and through small villages in an area of chalk upland bordering Cranborne Chase. Straddling the Dorset–Hampshire border, the region is rich in archeological remains and these will be the major points of interest. There are opportunities to inspect the remains of a Roman villa and the objects found, to observe a number of neolithic or Bronze Age burial mounds or barrows, and to admire and walk along the impressive Roman linear defensive earthworks of Bokerley Ditch and the less pronounced but clearly visible Grim's Ditch earthworks. From these earthworks it is possible to identify the section of the distant A354, which was formerly part of the Roman road stretching from Old Sarum to Dorchester. In addition and in contrast, visits can be made to the Heavy Horse Centre near Cripplestyle and the Craft Centre near Sandleheath.

Start (OS Landranger sheets 184 and 195. Grid reference for sheet 195: SU054132.)
Leave the Square in Cranborne, turn right at the junction with the B3708 and continue to the Fleur de Lys Inn. Turn left here along Castle Street in the direction of Alderholt.

Points of interest

▲ Cranborne: situated in Cranborne Chase, the hunting grounds of kings. The twelfth-century church stands on the site of an older one dating from the Benedictine priory of 980. The foundations of the Manor House, a former hunting lodge, are fourteenth century, but the house was refashioned in the seventeenth century. The Fleur de Lys Inn dates from the twelfth century and has included the poet Rupert Brooke among its guests.

Stage 1: Cranborne–Cripplestyle–Lower Daggons–Sandleheath

The road to Alderholt is flat with a good surface and runs alongside the River Crane past pleasant countryside. Landmarks to note are the watercress beds on the right approximately 1.5 miles from Cranborne and a pottery on the right at 2.5 miles, beyond which lies a garage, also on the right. Near this garage there is a sign to the Heavy Horse Centre. (Anyone wishing to visit the centre should turn right here and return to this point in order to continue the journey. The return trip will add an extra 2.5 miles to the ride.) From this signpost, continue in the direction of Alderholt and at the next signpost, in Cripplestyle, turn left towards Damerham.

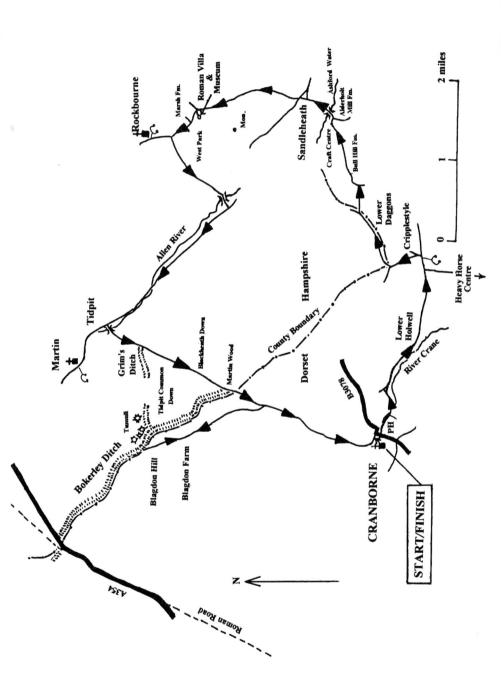

Rockbourne · Marsh Fm. · Roman Villa & Museum · West Park · Mon. · Sandleheath · Ashford Water · Craft Centre · Alderholt Mill Fm. · Bull Hill Fm. · Lower Daggons · Cripplestyle · Heavy Horse Centre · Hampshire · County Boundary · Dorset · Lower Holwell · River Crane · B3078 · PH · CRANBORNE · Allen River · Martin · Tidpit · Grim's Ditch · Blackheath Down · Martin Wood · Tidpit Common Down · Tumuli · Bokerley Ditch · Blagdon Hill · Blagdon Farm · A354 · Roman Road · N · 2 miles · 1 · 0

START/FINISH

48

This is a narrow switchback road which provides good views of Cranborne Chase and its woods and copses. Turn right at the sign to Lower Daggons (0.75 miles) and continue along this long straight road which runs just inside the Hampshire border. Pass through the small hamlet of Lower Daggons and turn right at the sign to Sandleheath. Cross a small bridge and climb the hill to Bull Hill Farm and continue to a T-junction near Alderholt Mill Farm and the Craft Centre. Turn left, cross over Ashford Water, climb the hill into Sandleheath and continue to the Give Way sign.

Points of interest

▲   The Dorset Heavy Horse Centre: preserves and breeds different heavy horses and has a variety of other horses and ponies. It also has aviaries and a collection of wildfowl. There is a café and picnic area. Open all year.

▲   Daggons (in Alderholt): the hamlet is named after the family of Richard Dagon, who lived here in the fourteenth century.

Stage 2: Sandleheath–Tidpit–Blagdon Farm–Cranborne

Go straight across the road and follow the sign to Rockbourne and the Roman villa and the Morley Hewitt Museum. This is a pleasant area for cycling. To the left, in West Park, a monument capped by a spherical dome can be seen.

On leaving the museum, turn left and rejoin the road to Rockbourne. Take the next turning on the left after Marsh Farm (on the right) to Damerham and Cranborne. The road passes the entrance to West Park and rises gently before dropping down to the River Allen. Cross over the river, disregard the sign to Damerham and at the next T-junction turn right towards Martin. You will soon see a sign on the left to Cranborne. Do not follow this sign but continue straight on alongside the River Allen towards Martin.

Turn left to Cranborne at the entrance to the village of Tidpit. Cross the river and look for signs of Grim's Ditch up on the ridge to the right. Carry on uphill to Tidpits Common and look for the noticeboard on the right which stands near a stile-gate. Pass through the gate and walk up to and over the field ridge to the point where the well-defined defensive ditch can be clearly seen.

Continue downhill through Martin Wood, which will take you back from Hampshire into Dorset. Turn right at the sign to Blagdon Farm and travel along a well-surfaced road past the farm to a point where the road becomes a hard track up through the woods to the summit of Blagdon Hill. Walk or ride up this track and at the fork bear right for a short distance until clear of the trees. There are tumuli at the summit as well as a fine view of Bokerley Ditch, stretching away down to and beyond the A354, part of the Roman road between Old Sarum and Dorchester. The point where Bokerley joins Grim's Ditch can also be seen.

Return to the road, turn right and follow the road back to the Square in Cranborne.

Points of interest

▲   West Park: the tall column in the park was erected by the East India Company to commemorate the capture of Pondicherry in 1761 by Sir Eyre Coote, who bought the West Park estate on his return from India. He is buried at Rockbourne.

▲ Bokerley Ditch: an impressive fourth-century Romano-British defence against Saxon invasion from the north-east. It begins south-east of Middle Chase Farm (OS Landranger sheet 184, grid reference SU003205) and ends on the Hampshire–Dorset border above the Hampshire village of Martin. It is now part of the Martin Down Nature Reserve.

▲ Grim's Ditch: a second supportive defensive ditch which links with Bokerley Ditch at Blagdon Hill. Sections of this ditch can be traced north-east of Rockbourne, on Tidpit Common, Blagdon Hill and linking the line of the Roman Road to the A354 at Swaynes Firs (OS Landranger sheet 184, grid reference SU067222).

Cranborne Manor

Ride 10

A TOUR IN NORTH-WEST DORSET

Distance: 18 miles **Journey time:** *approximately 3 hours*

Route Description

This ride explores an area of North-West Dorset which borders the neighbouring county of Somerset. It begins in Yetminster, wends its way to Melbury Osmond and crosses Melbury Park to Evershot and on to Corscombe, Halstock and Ryme Intrinsica before returning to Yetminster. Each village has distinct charm and is linked to its neighbours by a network of country lanes that offer woodland rides and wonderful scenic views. There are only two climbs of any consequence on this ride (up to the church in Melbury Osmond and through Adam's Green to Clarkham Cross), but they do not spoil an enjoyable ride.

Start *(OS Landranger sheet 194 Grid reference ST593105)*

The ride begins in Church Street, Yetminster, and passes Stonehouse Farm as it heads away from the centre of the village. It also passes a farmhouse called Upbury, on the right, which was the home of Benjamin Jesty (1736–1816), farmer and pioneer vaccinator against smallpox.

Follow the road as it bears to the right and up the hill to a junction with Birch Lane. Turn left. Where the road drops steeply to a bend and forks, bear right, taking the road to Melbury Osmond. This passes the Cuckoo Livery Service on the left on its way to a T-junction at a small triangle of land. Turn left and ride to the junction with the A37, the Yeovil to Dorchester road. Turn left and ride the short distance to the first turning on the right to Melbury Osmond.

Points of interest

▲ Yetminster: an interesting village with some fine seventeenth-century buildings, including an old grammar school founded by Robert Boyle, the famous scientist, in 1691. The bells of the fifteenth-century church chime 'God Save the Queen' every three hours to remind the village of Queen Victoria's Jubilee. Yetminster is the birthplace of farmer Benjamin Jesty, who introduced vaccination against smallpox by inoculating his family with cowpox in 1774.

Stage 1: *Melbury Osmond–Evershot–Benville*

Follow the road as it climbs past the church to a crossroads. Turn left, disregard the Dead End sign, pass the entrance to the churchyard and ride down the main street of the village. Cross the ford and ride up the hill to Town's End and the road across Melbury Park. Follow the road past Melbury House and across the deer park to the entrance gates near

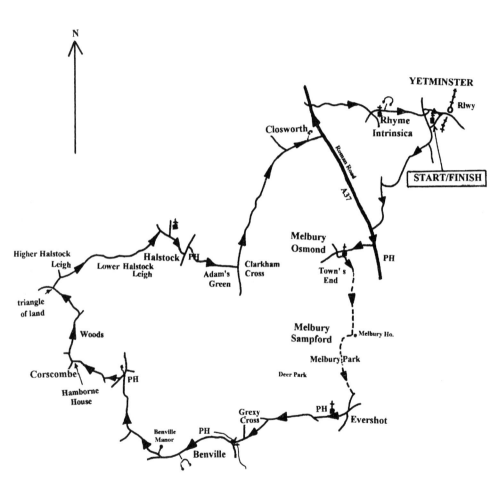

N

YETMINSTER

Rlwy

Rhyme
Intrinsica

Closworth

Roman Road

A37

START/FINISH

Melbury
Osmond

Higher Halstock
Leigh

Halstock

PH

Lower Halstock
Leigh

Adam's
Green

Clarkham
Cross

Town's
End

PH

triangle
of land

Melbury
Sampford

Melbury Ho.

Woods

Melbury Park

Corscombe

Deer Park

Hamborne
House

PH

PH

Grexy
Cross

PH

Evershot

Benville
Manor

PH

Benville

the village of Evershot. Take care on the downhill run to the gates, as there is a cattle grid between the gate pillars which cannot be seen until you are within a short distance of it.

Leave the park and turn right at the T-junction and ride into the village of Evershot. Pass the Acorn Inn, then climb out of the village. Ride straight on at Grexy Cross before running down to and crossing a bridge over a stream. Continue through the hamlet of Benville to the first turning on the right. Pass the entrance to Benville Manor and follow the narrow, winding road to a junction. Turn right and follow the road down to a junction near the Fox Inn. Turn sharp left and climb the hill to the first turning on the right. Follow this narrow lane to a T-junction. Turn right and ride through the delightful village of Corscombe.

Points of interest

▲ Melbury Osmond: a beautiful village with some fine thatched cottages and strong associations with Thomas Hardy. On the northern side of the church of St Osmond beyond the churchyard wall is a thatched cottage where Hardy's mother lived before her marriage. The stone house that stands opposite Clammer's Gate, the gateway to the park, in the part of the village known as Town's End was once the home of Hardy's grandparents.

▲ Melbury Sampford: the greater part of the manor house was built by Sir Giles Strangways in the sixteenth century and enlarged during the latter part of the seventeenth century. The church next to the house dates from the fifteenth century. Access is by foot or cycle through the park, passing the house, which is not open to the public.

▲ Evershot: a charming village, claiming to be the second highest in Dorset, it lies well-hidden in a hollow in the hills. In the nineteenth century raised pavements and bow fronts were added to buildings of an earlier era. The Acorn Inn provides refreshments. In a nearby wood can be found St John's Well, from which the Dorset River Frome rises.

▲ Corscombe: a long village with several old dwellings, among them The Fox Inn, which is 300 years old. Across from the inn is an old moated farmhouse and tithe barn. The village was associated with the Bloody Assizes of 1685, when a number of men were hanged after the Battle of Sedgemoor.

Stage 2: *Corscombe–Halstock–Closworth–Ryme Intrinsica–Yetminster*

Bear right at the junction in Corscombe near Hamborne House. Pass Knapp Farm, disregard the road on the left and carry straight on. This is a memorable ride down through a wood and across a bridge over a stream. There follows a short climb to a point where the road turns sharp left. Follow it to a junction at a small triangle of land and turn right to Halstock (2 miles). Carry straight on at the next junction, passing Wynford House and the Wynford Workshops on the left. This area is called Lower Halstock.

At the next T-junction turn right to Halstock. Turn left at the T-junction in the centre of the village, then first right along a lane that runs alongside the Quiet Woman Inn. Follow the sign to Closworth. The road runs between high hedges passing Portland House before running downhill, crossing a bridge and climbing through a heavily wooded area

The Fox Inn, Corscombe

to Adam's Green and a T-junction. Turn left and ride to Closworth and beyond to the junction with the A37. Turn left and then first right to Ryme Intrinsica. Bear left by Church Farm Cottage in the village and carry on to the road junction in Yetminster. Go straight across and return to Church Road.

Points of interest

▲ Halstock: the village stands astride the Harrow Way, one of the oldest roads in Britain. It is best known for the inn The Quiet Woman, with its inn-sign showing the lady holding her severed head under her arm. She is Jethwa, a noblewoman devoted to serving God, who was martyred when her brother Bana struck off her head. Legend has it that she picked up her head from the ground, carried it into church and placed it on the altar. There is also evidence of Iron Age and Roman occupation in the area.

▲ Ryme Intrinsica: a pleasant village renowned for its delightful name, which may be related to its close proximity to the Dorset–Somerset border.

Ride 11

THE FRIARY WAY

Distance: 25 miles Journey time: 5–6 hours

Route Description

The peaceful environment of the Friary of St Francis at Hilfield is one which the rider will experience on the first stage of the journey along the quiet roads from Yetminster to Gore Hill. As a reward for climbing this steep hill, there are spectacular views over the Blackmoor Vale and the wide chalk ridge, where there are carpets of bluebells in the spring. The flat pastureland and scattered farmsteads of the Vale contrast sharply with the undulating and seemingly uninhabited chalk uplands.

The long run down to Holywell is followed by a gentle climb to Evershot, a delightful village with charming houses and an excellent inn. Rampisham is quiet and attractive; its thatched cottages, church and manor house combine to give the impression of time standing still. From here the road winds its way alongside a tributary of the River Frome to Wraxall, Sandhills and Cattistock – a short but worthwhile deviation – before continuing the journey to Chalmington, Frome St Quintin and Holywell.

The final stage of the journey from Holywell to the Blackmoor Vale uses a minor road which runs round the base of Batcombe Hill and avoids a hill climb. The remainder of the ride through Chetnole and Hamlet to Yetminster ends what is an extremely pleasant cycle ride.

The route is suitable for riders of all abilities. Stage 2 can be omitted, making an equally pleasant but shorter ride.

Start (*OS Landranger sheet 194. Grid reference ST593105.*)

The ride begins from Church Street in Yetminster. Cycle down Church Street to the junction with the High Street and turn right. Follow the road past the railway station, across the railway bridge and bear right up the hill which leads out of the village.

Points of interest

▲ Yetminster: an interesting village with some fine seventeenth-century buildings, including an old grammar school founded by Robert Boyle, the famous scientist, in 1691. The bells of the fifteenth-century church chime 'God Save the Queen' every three hours to remind the village of Queen Victoria's Jubilee. Yetminster is the birthplace of Benjamin Jesty, the farmer who introduced vaccination against smallpox by inoculating his family with cowpox in 1774.

Stage 1: Yetminster–Leigh–Hilfield–Holywell

The road drops down from the top of the hill on the outskirts of Yetminster to a fork at

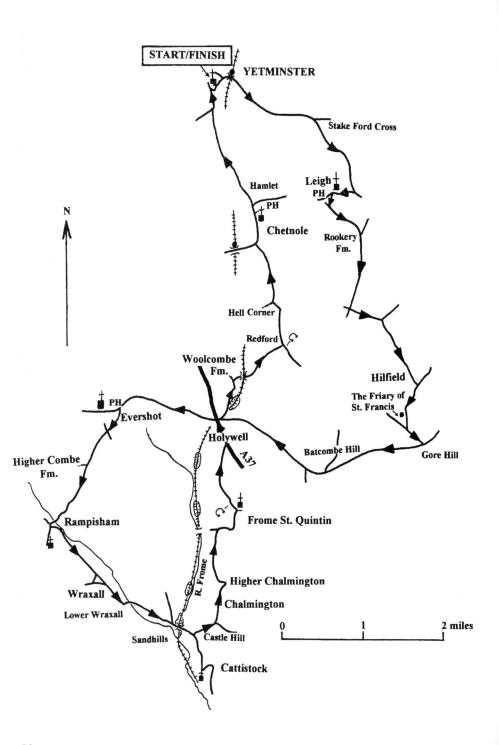

START/FINISH

YETMINSTER

Stake Ford Cross

N

Hamlet

Leigh
PH

Chetnole

PH

Rookery
Fm.

Hell Corner

Redford

Woolcombe
Fm.

Hilfield

The Friary of
St. Francis

PH
Evershot

Holywell

A37

Batcombe Hill

Gore Hill

Higher Combe
Fm.

Rampisham

Frome St. Quintin

R. Frome

Higher Chalmington

Chalmington

Wraxall

Lower Wraxall

Sandhills

Castle Hill

0   1   2 miles

Cattistock

Stake Ford Cross. Bear right to Leigh and follow the road to the village cross, sited at the junction of two roads. Turn right by the cross, and take the first turning on the left beyond the church and opposite The Carpenters Arms public house. Ride along this lane, which runs through a housing area to a T-junction opposite Pound Farm. Turn left and at the next T-junction turn right. Rookery Farm is on the right.

Continue to a crossroads and turn left towards Hermitage and Hilfield Church. This road is narrow but has a good surface. At a fork bear right to Hilfield. The road twists its way downhill before passing Knapp House and on through Hilfield. At the next T-junction turn right towards the Friary of St Francis. This narrow and rather poorly surfaced road leads down to and past the Friary, from where it rises to a road junction.

Bear left onto a minor road that rises quite steeply between dense wooded banks to a T-junction at the summit of Gore Hill. Turn right towards Batcombe Hill and Holywell. Disregard the turns to Batcombe and Maiden Newton and follow the ridge road down to the Yeovil to Dorchester road (the A37). Turn right onto the A37 and then almost immediately left to join the road to Evershot. It may be safer to walk across this junction.

Points of interest
▲ Leigh: a quiet village with many attractive old cottages and hamstone houses. It has three stone crosses and in a field south of the village there is the trace of a medieval ground maze called a 'mizmaze'.
▲ Hilfield: the home of the Franciscan monks who started a 'Home for Young Vagrants' after the 1914–18 war. Their church is mainly fifteenth century and contains beautiful wood carvings, the work of seventeenth-century Flemish craftsmen.

Stage 2: Holywell–Evershot–Rampisham–Wraxall–Cattistock–Chalmington–Frome St Quintin–Holywell

---

Cross the railway bridge, skirt the village of Holywell and climb the gently sloping hill towards Evershot. From the summit the road runs down into the village of Evershot, passing Rose Cottage on the left and the exit road from Melbury Park on the right, which emerges at a triangular area of grassed land known as the Common. It can be identified by the unusual stone seat with a wooden base. From here the road rises through the main street of the village. Take the first turning on the left to Cattistock and Rampisham.

The road climbs past the Summer Lodge County House Hotel and Restaurant on the right to a crossroads. Go directly ahead and follow the road past Higher Combe Farm and down into the village of Rampisham. Pass the thatched post office and turn left to Wraxall and Cattistock, where four roads meet at a triangle of land.

Follow the road to Wraxall as it wends its way alongside and above the tributary of the River Frome. Disregard the turning to Higher Wraxall and keep straight on to Lower Wraxall and from there to Sandhills and Cattistock. Cross the railway bridge in Sandhills and ride to a signposted junction. To visit Cattistock, bear right and ride the half-mile into the centre of this interesting village. Then return to the signposted junction and bear right to resume the journey to Chalmington and Frome St Quintin.

The red-brick house at Frome St Quintin

This straight road runs towards a wood, where the road forks. Turn left to Chalmington. Within a short distance the road passes the entrance to Chalmington House and Chalmington Farm, before dropping down to Higher Chalmington and a sharp left-hand bend. From here the road rises steeply round a right-hand bend before levelling out to provide open views across to Chantmarle House to the north-west. Pass the entrance drive to the house and carry on through Frome St Quentin to the junction with the A37. Turn left to Holywell and take the first turning on the right towards Batcombe.

Points of interest

▲ Evershot: a charming village, claiming to be the second highest village in Dorset, it lies well hidden in a hollow in the hills. It was largely rebuilt in the nineteenth century, when raised pavements and bow fronts were added to buildings of an earlier era. The Acorn Inn provides refreshments. In a nearby wood is St John's Well, from which rises the River Frome.

▲ Rampisham: a straggling village with a thatched post office set close to a delightful stream and an old, moss-covered bridge. Four roads meet just below the church, which has fierce-looking gargoyles and a sixteenth-century stone cross in the churchyard with carvings depicting the martyrdoms of Thomas à Becket, St Edmund and St Peter and the stoning of Stephen, among others.

▲ Cattistock: an interesting village with a rich mixture of old and new houses, a post office and the Fox and Hounds Inn. The magnificent tower of the church is the result of extensive work which took place in the last century by George Scott and his son, Sir Giles Gilbert Scott. Its other features include a twelfth-century-style clock and a window by William Morris.

▲　Frome St Quintin: a charming little village with a fine eighteenth-century red-brick house set in gracious grounds. An unusual hedge fronts the house.

Stage 3: Holywell–Redford–Chetnole–Hamlet–Yetminster

Take the first left turn on the Batcombe Road after leaving the A37. This is a narrow road which runs past the entrance to Woolcombe Farm before passing under the railway bridge and continuing to a road junction at Redford. Bear left and follow the road through Chetnole, passing the Chetnole Inn before riding on to Hamlet. From here the journey continues to Yetminster by way of Tarks Hill. Bear right for Yetminster at the fork situated a little way up the short but steep incline of Tarks Hill.

Ride 12

THE COUNTRYSIDE
AROUND CERNE ABBAS

Distance: 17.5 miles Journey time: 3–4 hours

Route Description

The ride begins in the quiet and attractive village of Leigh and follows the quiet lanes of the Blackmoor Vale to the foot of the chalk ridge which separates the valley of the River Cerne from the neighbouring valley of the River Piddle. The peaceful countryside around Hermitage, Holnest Park and Glanvilles Wootton consists of fairly flat, rich pastureland dotted with many attractive farmhouses of Tudor or Jacobean origin.

The only serious climb is that to the summit of the chalk ridge. This starts from the road junction near Middlemarsh, the gradient being gentle as far as Lower Revels Farm but increasing after that. There are spectacular views from the summit of the ridge, followed by a swift and exciting ride down to Cerne Abbas. This village, which lies at the heart of Dorset, has much of interest to offer the visitor.

From Cerne Abbas the ride briefly joins the A352, where the Cerne Giant can be seen on the hillside, then continues to Up Cerne. The A352 is then rejoined for the journey through Minterne Magna to a minor road that leads across the vale to the crossroads near Hermitage and back to Leigh.

This is a ride where the majority of the terrain is fairly flat and the average rider should not be deterred at the prospect of the climb to the chalk ridge; it is such a short distance compared with the easy riding of the rest of the journey.

Start (OS Landranger sheet 194. Grid reference ST621084.)

From the stone cross at the road junction in Leigh, ride in a westerly direction towards the church and take the first turning on the left just beyond the church, and opposite The Carpenters Arms public house. This narrow lane passes between a mixture of new and old houses before arriving at at T-junction. Turn left and at the next T-junction turn right. Pass Rookery Farm with its lovely thatched farmhouse on the right and at the crossroads turn left to Hermitage.

Points of interest

▲ Leigh: a quiet village with many attractive old cottages and hamstone houses. It has three stone crosses and in a field south of the village there are traces of a medieval ground maze called a 'mizmaze'.

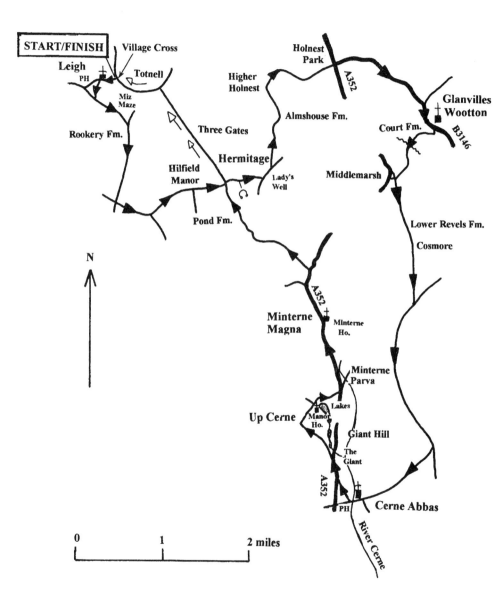

START/FINISH

Leigh
PH
Village Cross
Totnell
Miz Maze

Rookery Fm.

Three Gates

Hilfield Manor

Pond Fm.

Hermitage

Lady's Well

Higher Holnest

Holnest Park

A352

Almshouse Fm.

Glanvilles Wootton

B3146

Court Fm.

Middlemarsh

Lower Revels Fm.

Cosmore

N

Minterne Magna

Minterne Ho.

Minterne Parva

Up Cerne

Lakes

Manor Ho.

Giant Hill

The Giant

A352

PH

Cerne Abbas

River Cerne

A352

0   1   2 miles

The road to Hermitage is narrow with a good surface. At the fork bear left to Hermitage. The road runs downhill before climbing past Hilfield Manor and on to crossroads. Turn left and then immediately right to Hermitage (0.75 miles). The road runs straight and downhill. Keep bearing left at each junction in this small straggling village. Beyond the village the road twists and turns along a flat road, passing Almshouse Farm, before it rises gradually along a well-surfaced road flanked on both sides by woodland. It passes Holnest Lodge, which stands high to the left, and crosses the parkland to the Give Way sign at the junction with the A352.

Turn right and then immediately left along the B3146 to Glanvilles Wootton. Follow this road as it passes through Osehill Green and at the junction in Glanvilles Wootton bear right with the B3146. Pass the war memorial and the entrance to the churchyard and leave the B3146 at the next turning on the right, near Court Farm. This minor road leads to Middlemarsh, sweeping away to the right before straightening out. It crosses a bridge over a stream and continues to a Give Way sign. Turn left along a road which rises gently to Lower Revels Farm, beyond which the incline becomes steeper as it makes its way to

The Abbot's Hall, Cerne Abbas

the summit of the chalk ridge. This is the longest hill of the whole journey. Bear right where a road joins from the left. Just beyond this junction the summit of the ridge is reached and the road becomes flat. Take the first turning on the right to Cerne Abbas and follow the road down into the village.

Points of interest

▲   Holnest: noted for its parkland and Holnest Lodge.

▲   Cerne Abbas: an old and interesting village with some beautiful architecture and attractive inns. The gatehouse, with its magnificent oriel window, the guest house and the tithe barn are all that remain of the tenth-century abbey. The famous Cerne Giant lies on the hillside outside the village, 180 feet tall and carrying a 120-foot club in his 7-foot-long fingers. There is a path to the giant from the village.

Stage 2: Cerne Abbas–Up Cerne–Minterne Magna–Three Gates–Totnell–Leigh

Ride along the main street of Cerne Abbas to the New Inn and turn right down Duck Street, which is directly opposite the inn. The road leads uphill, passing the picnic area on the right before reaching a junction with the A352. There is an excellent view of the Cerne Abbas Giant near this point.

Turn right onto the A352 and take the first road on the left to Up Cerne. Follow this minor road across this pastureland and bear right with the road, passing the manor house and church, which are to the right. The road dips down as it passes through the hamlet before climbing through the woods to the junction with the A352.

Turn left and ride through Minterne Magna, then take the second turning on the left, near an old school building with a bell tower. Follow this road as it winds its way through woods and open country to the crossroads near Pond Farm. Keep straight ahead at the crossroads, passing through Three Gates and Totnell before returning to Leigh.

Points of interest

▲ Minterne Magna: a delightful village, it was once the home of the great families of the Napiers (Sir Nathaniel built the almshouses in Dorchester), the Churchills and the Digbys, who still own the manor house. The manor gardens are famous for their rhododendrons.

Ride 13

A RIDE THROUGH THE TARRANT VILLAGES

Distance: 18 miles Journey time: 3–4 hours

Route Description

This is an easy ride. It begins from the car park of the Sunrise Business Park near Blandford Forum, and heads north along the Shaftesbury road to join a minor road to Tarrant Gunville. Within a short distance this minor road passes Harbin's Park, a medieval deer park hidden in the woods near by. The route then leads to Tarrant Gunville, the northernmost of the Tarrant villages. The valley deepens and narrows on its approach to Tarrant Rawston and Tarrant Rushton, taking the rider beneath the steep chalk hill called The Cliff. The scenery along the meandering river is varied and interesting. From Tarrant Crawford the route takes the rider to Langton Long Blandford and Blandford Forum before returning to the starting point in the car park.

Start (OS Landranger sheets 194 and 195. Grid reference ST888082.)

The ride begins from the car park in the Sunrise Business Park, which is situated near the A350 roundabout to Blandford Forum. On leaving the car park turn right and ride for about 2.25 miles before reaching the signposted right turn to Tarrant Gunville. The road runs alongside a dense wood before dropping steeply to a sharp left turn into a hollow flanked by trees. Climb out of the hollow and ride the short distance to a signposted bridlepath on the left near a barn. Approximately 300 yards along this path there is a good view of Harbin's Park, a fine medieval deer park. The journey continues along the road from the signpost down past Westbury Farm to a T-junction. Turn left and follow the road to a T-junction in Tarrant Gunville. Turn right into the village.

Points of interest

▲ Harbin's Park: a medieval deer park covering 115 acres. It is completely enclosed by a large bank with an internal ditch and is one of the most secret and best-preserved deer parks in Dorset.

Stage 1: *Tarrant Gunville–Tarrant Hinton–Tarrant Launceston–Tarrant Monkton*

Pass the church on the right and the entrance to Eastbury House on the left before riding on to Tarrant Hinton and the junction with the A354. Turn right onto the A354 and then almost immediately left to Tarrant Launceston and Tarrant Monkton. Pass through the hamlet of Tarrant Launceston and at Tarrant Monkton enter the village either by a foot-

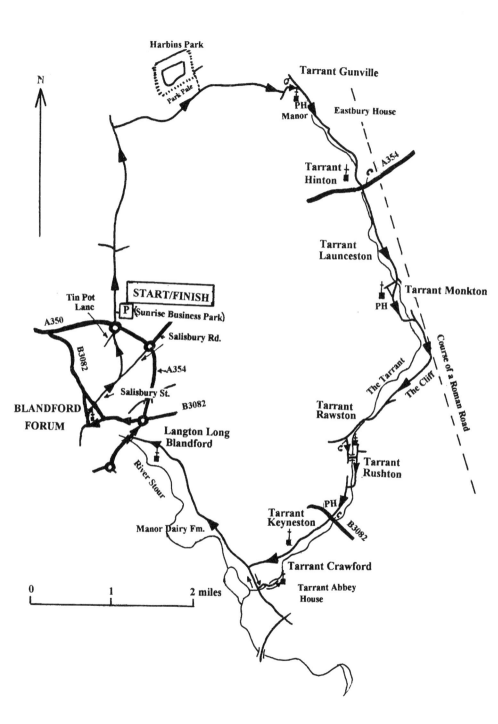

Harbins Park

Tarrant Gunville

Park Pale

PH
Manor

Eastbury House

N

Tarrant
Hinton

A354

Tarrant
Launceston

Tin Pot
Lane

START/FINISH

P (Sunrise Business Park)

A350

Salisbury Rd.

Tarrant Monkton

PH

B3082

A354

Salisbury St.

The Tarrant

Course of a Roman Road

The Cliff

BLANDFORD
FORUM

B3082

Langton Long
Blandford

Tarrant
Rawston

River Stour

Tarrant
Rushton

Manor Dairy Fm.

Tarrant
Keyneston

PH

C

B3082

Tarrant Crawford

0   1   2 miles

Tarrant Abbey
House

bridge over the Tarrant or by riding through the ford. Ride through this delightful village, bearing left by the Langton Arms. Pass Manor Farm, cross the bridge over the river and turn right to Tarrant Rawston at the T-junction.

Points of interest
▲ Tarrant Gunville: the northernmost of the Tarrant villages. It contains some attractive cottages and the one remaining wing of the once imposing mansion in Eastbury Park. The mansion, built in 1738 to a design by Sir John Vanbrugh, is said to have rivalled Blenheim Palace. Most of the building was demolished in 1795. There is a memorial plaque in the church in memory of Thomas Wedgewood FRS, third son of Josiah Wedgewood of Etruria, the potter; he died in 1805 aged 34, and was buried here. Thomas Wedgewood is chiefly remembered for his work in photography. Although he failed to discover a practical photographic process, he is credited with conceiving the idea of utilizing the chemical action of light to making pictures, either by contact or in the camera.
▲ Tarrant Monkton: a picturesque village complete with thatched cottages, a packhorse bridge and a ford.

Stage 2: Tarrant Monkton–Tarrant Rawston–Tarrant Rushton–Tarrant Keyneston–Tarrant Crawford

---

This section of the road to Tarrant Rawston runs towards the course of the Roman road from Old Sarum, near Salisbury, to Badbury Rings. It is closest at the point where the road

Tarrant Abbey House, Tarrant Crawford

turns sharp right and runs below a high bank called The Cliff. Cross the river bridge and at the fork in Tarrant Rawston bear left to Tarrant Rushton. Take the first left turn up to the village of Tarrant Rushton and at the T-junction turn left to St Mary's Church. From the church return to the T-junction and follow the road through the village. It eventually bears right and leads to a bridge over the river and the original road. Dismount and wheel your bicycle across this narrow footbridge.

Continue left along this road to the T-junction with the B3082 near the True Lovers Knot Inn in Tarrant Keyneston. Go straight across the road and ride through this delightful village. At the next T-junction turn left and ride to the entrance which leads to St Mary's Church in Tarrant Crawford. This entrance is situated at a point on the left just before the road crosses a bridge over the river. Although it is signposted as a private drive, access to the church is allowed. The drive sweeps past the front of Tarrant Abbey House and alongside farm buildings to the church entrance. Retrace the path back to the road and turn right up the hill.

Points of interest
▲ Tarrant Rushton: a small village set back from the valley road. St Mary's Church is well worth a visit.

Stage 3: *Tarrant Crawford–Langton Long Blandford–Blandford Forum–Sunrise Trading Estate*

Ride up the hill past Keynston Mill and Fruit Farm on the left, and continue straight on to Langton Long Blandford. Turn right at the T-junction with the A354, ride up to the roundabout and turn left down Wimborne Road. Follow its continuation, East Street, into the centre of the town. Pass the church on the right and turn right up Salisbury Street. At the fork follow the Salisbury Road to the traffic lights. Go straight ahead along Shaftesbury Road, past the police station, and turn left along Shaftesbury Lane at the sign to Shaftesbury and Melbury Abbas. Continue past the industrial estate on the left and at the T-junction with Tin Pot Lane bear right to the roundabout on the A354 and return to the Sunrise Trading Estate.

Points of interest
▲ Tarrant Crawford: the present village lies half a mile south-east of the site of the original village, of which only the old parish church, a farm and its outbuildings remain. The original village may have been moved to its present site to make way for the Cistercian nunnery which was established in 1230. The church dates from the twelfth century and contains many interesting features, most notable being the fourteenth-century wall paintings.
▲ Blandford Forum: a good example of an eighteenth-century market town. Its most prominent building is the Church of St Peter and St Paul, built during the years 1732 to 1739 to the design of William and John Bastard.

Ride 14

FROM BEAMINSTER TO EGGARDON HILL AND BRIDPORT

Distance: 23 miles *Journey time:* approximately 6 hours

Route Description

Beaminster is the starting point for a ride which follows the course of the River Hooke from the village of Hooke to Toller Porcorum. Here it leaves this quiet, rather mysterious river valley and climbs gradually through open countryside to the large hill fort of Eggardon Hill. From this high point there follows a long exhilarating run downhill to Powerstock. The remaining journey takes the rider through Nettlecombe, Loders and Bradpole before briefly joining the A35(T) and the main road through Bridport.

The minor road to Beaminster (Victoria Grove) leaves the main road (West Street) in Bridport and follows the River Brit through Pymore, Wooth, Waytown and Netherbury before returning to the A3066 and Beaminster.

Apart from a climb up Storridge Hill and another from Toller Porcorum to Eggardon Hill, the route is free from steep hills. The continually varying landscape together with the attractive villages make this an enjoyable ride.

Start *(OS Landranger sheets 193 and 194. Grid reference for sheet 193: ST481013.)*

From the public car park in Beaminster turn left into Fleet Street, bearing left at the fork in the road. At the Halt sign turn left onto the A3066 and follow the road downhill, turning left along Whitcombe Road (the B3163). The road is signposted to Dorchester, Evershot and Maiden Newton.

Points of interest

▲ Beaminster: a charming town of interesting hamstone buildings grouped around the market square. Nearby Parnham House, an attractive Tudor building, is now home to the John Makepeace Workshop, which holds monthly exhibitions of finely crafted furniture.

Stage 1: Beaminster–Hooke–Toller Porcorum–Eggardon Hill

The road rises and then falls prior to a climb up Storridge Hill. Take the second turning on the right along the signposted road to Hooke.

Disregard the first turning on the left to Toller Whelme and continue along the edge of Hooke Park wood to the next turning on the left to Hooke. The road drops steeply through the wood, passing the entrance to Hooke Court and continuing alongside the River Hooke to the church of St Giles, near a crossroads in the centre of the village. Go straight ahead

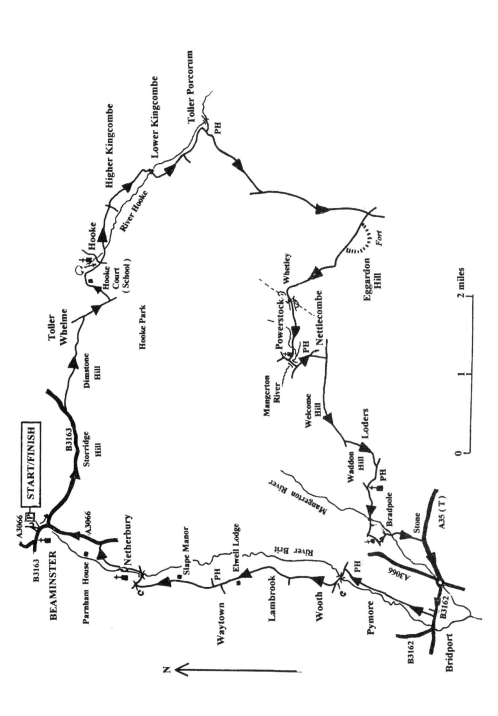

69

at the crossroads, along Kingscombe Road. The road passes through Higher Kingscombe and over the river at Lower Kingscombe before arriving at a signpost to Toller Porcorum. Continue straight ahead and turn right at the T-junction (the Old Swan Inn is near by). Pass the village stores/post office and the church of St Andrew and St Peter and climb out of the village to a T-junction. Turn left towards Askerswell.

The road rises gradually. At the next crossroads turn right towards Powerstock and West Milton, along a road designated as unsuitable for heavy goods vehicles. Part of the defensive ditches of the hill fort run parallel to it.

To visit Eggardon Hill and the fortifications, look for a single gate in the boundary fence on the left a short distance along the Powerstock road. The gate opens onto a well-defined footpath leading across the field to the hill and fortifications. Bicycles can be wheeled across quite easily. A visit to this hill fort is highly recommended.

Points of interest

▲ Hooke: a small, quiet and pleasant hamlet on the River Hooke. Hooke Court, the seventeenth-century manor house, is now a study centre.

▲ Toller Porcorum: Toller is the original name of the River Hooke and means 'a stream in a valley'. Porcorum means 'of the pigs' and refers to the time when pigs were woodland animals and lived for much of the autumn on beechmast and acorns.

▲ Eggardon Hill: this impressive Iron Age hill fort, 828 feet high, with an intricate system of earthworks, offers breathtaking views over the surrounding landscape.

Parnham House

From Eggardon Hill return to the Powerstock road. It descends steeply to a sharp left-hand bend at Whetley, then crosses a disused railway bridge and a small brook before entering Powerstock. Follow the road past the church of St Mary the Virgin to the junction at the centre of the village, and follow the signposted direction to Bridport. Cross the Mangerton River and at the next T-junction turn left to Nettlecombe.

Bear right at the fork near the Marquis of Lorne Public House and turn right at the next T-junction. Follow the road and take the left turn to Loders which leads around the base of Waddon Hill to the T-junction in the village. Turn right and continue through Loders and at the junction outside the village follow the signposted direction to Bridport. Cross the Mangerton River and turn left into Bradpole. Pass the church and take the first turn on the left. Ride down through a housing estate to a bridge over the Mangerton River and from there to Stone and a T-junction with the A35(T) Bridport–Dorchester road. Turn right and at the roundabout follow the B3162 (East Street) into the centre of Bridport.

Continue along the main street to Victoria Grove, a turning on the right just beyond the traffic lights near the Arts Centre and Museum. Ride along Victoria Grove to Pymore and on to a T-junction. Turn left towards Dottery and at the fork in the road turn right towards Wooth, Waytown and Netherbury.

Points of interest

▲ Powerstock: the village lies at the foot of Eggardon hill fort and not far from the hilltop known as Powerstock Castle. The twelfth-century church has an outstanding Norman chancel arch. Another treasure is the ancient dole table in the churchyard, on which loaves of bread were placed for distribution to the poor.

▲ Bridport: a market town with wide pavements once used for stretching nets and ropes. It has many historical associations; for example, Charles II once escaped Cromwell's soldiers at the George Inn (now a chemist's shop).

Stage 3: Wooth–Waytown–Netherbury–Beaminster

From Wooth the road runs through pleasant countryside to the village of Waytown with its cluster of attractive houses and the Hare and Hounds Inn. It then climbs past Slape Manor before arriving in Netherbury. At the crossroads in the village turn right and follow the road to Beaminster (1.5 miles). The road passes over the River Brit before arriving at a junction. Turn left along the road which runs parallel to the river. It passes an entrance to Parnham House and bears right to a T-junction with the A3066 Bridport–Beaminster road. Turn left and continue the short distance to Beaminster and the car park.

Points of interest

▲ Netherbury: a quiet village of honey-coloured stone straddling the River Brit. The fifteenth-century church contains memorial brasses to the seafaring Hood family.

Ride 15

FROM BEAMINSTER TO BROADWINDSOR, FORDE ABBEY AND STOKE ABBOTT

Distance: 22 miles Journey time: approximately 6 hours

Route Description

The tour begins in the busy little market town of Beaminster and climbs to Broadwindsor before taking to the quiet lanes which link Burstock, Childhay, Kittwhistle and Forde Abbey. From here the journey continues through Thorncombe and Birdsmoorgate to a point directly below the hill fort of Pilsdon Pen, the highest point in Dorset. From this hill there are panoramic views to the south across the Marshwood Vale and the coast. The route then runs into the Marshwood Vale to the village of Pilsdon and on to Shave Cross. There follows a steady climb from Blackeney to the rim of the vale and the final run down through the exquisite village of Stoke Abbott to Beaminster and the car park.

Delightful villages and quiet lanes set in a beautiful part of Dorset make this an enchanting ride, one that will draw the rider back again to explore more of its charms.

Start (OS Landranger sheet 193. Grid reference ST481013.)

From the exit to the public car park in Beaminster turn left into Fleet Street, bearing left at the fork in the road. At the Halt sign turn right into the town square and proceed along Hogshill Street in the signposted direction of Crewkerne and Broadwindsor.

Stage 1: *Beaminster–Broadwindsor–Burstock–Kittwhistle–Forde Abbey*

Turn left along Clay Lane (the B3163) to Broadwindsor, passing the Knapp Inn on the left. From Lower Barrowfield Farm the road rises in a stepped ascent, followed by a descent before the final climb to the outskirts of Broadwindsor near a craft centre on the left. Follow the one-way system into the centre of Broadwindsor and take the B3164 to Lyme Regis.

Take the first right turn to Burstock. The road runs downhill past Pound Cottage and on through the village of Burstock with Manor Farm on the left. Keep straight on at the next crossroads and take the next turning on the left to Childhay. The road rises from the junction and bears right by the manor house before passing over the Temple Brook.

Take the next unsignposted road on the right beyond the brook and proceed to Kittwhistle. Continue along this road until it meets the B3165, Crewkerne to Lyme Regis road. Turn right and then first left along a minor road towards Thorncombe. At the T-junction turn right in the signposted direction of Winsham and Chard. At the next T-junction turn left onto the B3162.

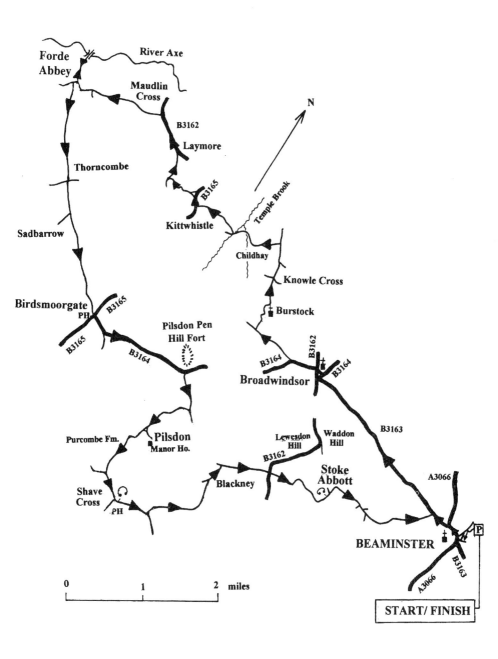

Forde Abbey

River Axe

Maudlin Cross

Thorncombe

B3162

Laymore

Sadbarrow

B3165

Temple Brook

Kittwhistle

Childhay

Knowle Cross

Birdsmoorgate
PH

B3165

B3165

B3164

Pilsdon Pen
Hill Fort

Burstock

B3164

B3162

B3164

Broadwindsor

Purcombe Fm.

Pilsdon
Manor Ho.

Lewesdon
Hill

Waddon
Hill

B3163

Shave
Cross
PH

B3162

Blackney

Stoke
Abbott

A3066

BEAMINSTER

P

A3066

B3163

N

0   1   2   miles

START/ FINISH

Pass the Squirrel Inn on the left, travel downhill and take the first turning on the left to Forde Abbey and Gardens at Maudlin Cross. The road passes Forde Grange on the left before dropping to a sharp left-hand bend. Here there is a division of roads, with a minor road going straight ahead and downhill to the entrance to Forde Abbey and Gardens, while the main road for the route bears left. Those wishing to visit the abbey should return to this sharp bend and continue the journey as described in the notes for the following stage.

Points of interest

▲ Beaminster: a delightful town, small and unspoilt, lying in a hollow at the head of a valley at the meeting point of four streams. The central market square, overlooked by the sixteenth-century Ham Hill stone tower of St Mary's Church, forms the focal point of the town. Other attractions include some fine Georgian houses and picturesque seventeenth-century almshouses.

▲ Broadwindsor: a large and attractive village which gave refuge to Charles II in September 1651 after the defeat of his army at Worcester. A plaque on the wall of a cottage in the centre of the village commemorates the occasion and marks the site of the inn where he was sheltered by a royalist innkeeper.

▲ Forde Abbey: a Cistercian monastery, founded in 1138, set beside the River Axe. It is now a private residence and houses the famous Mortlake Tapestries. The 30 acres of garden are open all year round. The house is open from March to October.

The house in Broadwindsor, formerly an inn, where Charles II took refuge

Follow the road round the sharp left-hand bend and take the first turning on the left to Birdsmoorgate. Go straight ahead at the next crossroads, passing Sadborow on the right, to the crossroads at Birdsmoorgate. Go straight across to join the B3164 to Broadwindsor.

Ride to a point directly beneath the hill fort on Pilsdon Pen and turn right at the signpost to Pilsdon. Follow the road down and at the fork turn right for Pilsdon, a small hamlet in the Marshwood Vale. In the village the road forks at a white-painted thatched cottage. Bear right to Shaves Cross. To see the manor house bear left at this fork, returning here to continue the journey to Shaves Cross.

The road to Shaves Cross rises from this fork and passes Purcombe Farm, over the brow of the hill. Turn left at the T-junction and continue through the hamlet of Shaves Cross, passing the Shave Cross Inn on the right. Take the next junction on the left to Stoke Abbott and Beaminster. Pass Lower Monkwood Farm on the right and continue to Blackney, from where the road climbs to the B3162. Go straight across to join the minor road which runs down to the village of Stoke Abbott. Pass through the village and return to Beaminster.

Points of interest

▲   Birdsmoorgate: a collection of houses and an inn around a crossroads. To the north of the inn is Racedown House, where William Wordsworth and his sister Dorothy lived for some time.

▲   Pilsdon Pen: Dorset's highest point (at 909 feet), with the ramparts and ditches of an Iron Age settlement on its summit. Commands wonderful views over the countryside and the coast.

▲   Pilsdon: a small attractive village with a manor nestling in the Marshwood Vale below Pilsdon Pen.

▲   Stoke Abbott: a beautiful village set in a deep cutting beneath three hills. One of these, Waddon Hill, is the site of a Roman fort.

Ride 16

A CIRCULAR TOUR FROM WIMBORNE MINSTER

Distance: 23 miles Journey time: approximately 4 hours

Route Description

The ride begins from Wimborne Minster and heads out on the (B3078) Cranborne Road. After crossing the Walford Bridge over the River Allen the route leaves the B3078 and continues through shaded lanes to the sandy heathland of Holt Heath. From here there are panoramic views over large areas of eastern Dorset. The heathland gives way to fields and woods near Horton Heath, while between Horton and Witchampton the landscape changes to rolling farmland as the wooded areas decrease in both size and number.

The villages and hamlets with their thatched cottages and beautiful gardens provide a constant source of pleasure and, together with the many points of historical interest, make this an interesting ride for cyclists of all abilities.

Start *(OS Landranger sheet 195. Grid reference SU006000.)*

In Wimborne Minster, leave the public car park in Old Road and turn right into Victoria Road (the B3082). At the mini-roundabout, turn left along West Street. Turn left by the King's Head Hotel and through the traffic lights, continuing out of town along the B3078 to Cranborne. Cross the Walford Bridge, over the River Allen, and take the third turning on the right. This is Burts Hill, where the road rises steadily to its summit near the Horns Inn.

Carry straight on to Broom Hill, disregarding the turning to Dumpton School. At the fork take the road to the right and at the T-junction turn left. Then take the first turning on the right along a narrow lane to Merry Field Hill. Pass Long Lane farm on the left and follow the road as it gently falls to a junction near the Barley Mow Inn. Turn left at this junction and at the crossroads in Broom Hill turn left to Holt. At the next junction bear right to God's Blessing Green and Holt.

Points of interest

⚲ Wimborne Minster: an ancient market town situated on the River Stour, its recorded history dates back to the eighth century. The Minster's principal points of interest include the lantern tower, an 800-year-old font and a chained library. Other interesting buildings near by are the thirteenth-century St Margaret's Hospital chapel and the Priest's House, a sixteenth-century building which is now the town's museum.

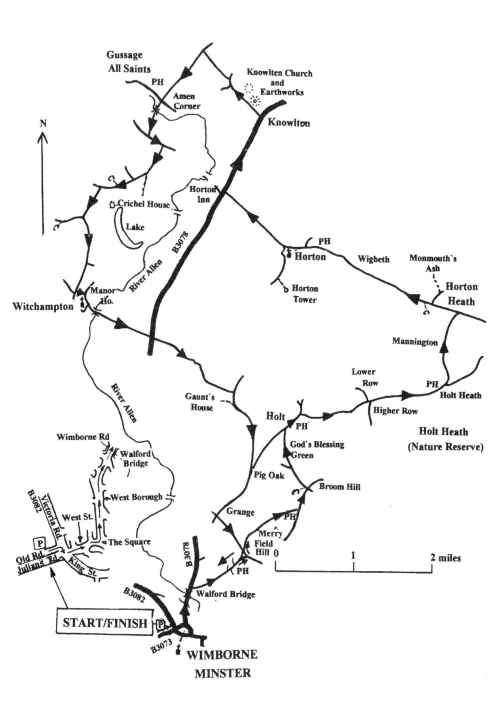

Gussage
All Saints

PH

Amen
Corner

Knowlten Church
and
Earthworks

Knowlton

Crichel House

Lake

Horton
Inn

PH

Horton

Wigbeth

Monmouth`s
Ash

Horton
Heath

N

River Allen

B3078

Witchampton

Manor
Ho.

Horton
Tower

Mannington

Lower
Row

PH

Holt Heath

Gaunt`s
House

Holt

Higher Row

Holt Heath
(Nature Reserve)

Wimborne Rd

Walford
Bridge

West Borough

PH

God`s Blessing
Green

Pig Oak

Broom Hill

River Allen

B3082

Victoria Rd

West St.

P

The Square

Grange

PH

Old Rd.
Julians Rd.

King St.

B3078

Merry
Field
Hill

0

1

2 miles

START/FINISH

P

B3082

PH

Walford Bridge

B3073

WIMBORNE
MINSTER

77

Pass through God's Blessing Green before entering the village of Holt alongside its large village green. The route passes Vicarage Farm on the right and the village green on the left. At the next junction turn right towards Horton. Pass the Olde Inn on the right.

Follow the road down from the inn and take the first turning on the right to Higher Row. Cross over a stream and pass Home Farm on the right before climbing up to a crossroads on the heathland of the Holt Heath Nature Reserve. Ride straight ahead across the heathland, passing the Cross Keys Inn in the village of Holt Heath. Bear left to Mannington at the next fork. The road runs downhill to a ford and on through the village to a T-junction at Horton Heath. Turn left to Horton (2.5 miles). Pass the picturesque Druscilla public house on the right before entering the village of Horton. Up to the left is the Horton Tower.

From Horton follow the road to a Give Way sign at the junction with the B3078. Turn right, pass the Horton Inn, and take the first turning on the left at Knowlton. Knowlton's church and earthworks are on the right. Continue along this road past Brockington Farm to the T-junction. Turn left and ride straight ahead at the crossroads at Amen Corner.

Points of interest

▲ Horton: there are some very picturesque cottages and a medieval manor house here. Horton Tower, built as an observatory in 1700 by Humphrey Sturt, stands 120 feet high, overlooking the village. It is now a ruin. Following the Battle of Sedgemoor in Somerset in 1685, the Duke of Monmouth escaped from the field of battle but was caught hiding in a ditch near Horton Heath. Above the ditch there was an ash tree, which became known as the Monmouth Ash; its location is marked.

▲ Knowlton: the Norman church lies approximately 300 yards from the now deserted village of Knowlton. It remains a mystery why it was built within the encircling bank and ditch of a prehistoric 'henge' or ritual monument constructed in about 2500 BC.

Stage 2: Gussage All Saints–More Crichel–Witchampton–Wimborne Minster

The road runs down to and over a stream before climbing to a T-junction. Turn left and then first right to More Crichel. Pass through the gates of the estate, disregard the minor farm road to the right and ride to a fork. Bear left and follow the road towards Witchampton.

Pass through the village and take the second turning on the left. This passes between the church, on the right, and the manor house, on the left. Bear left at the fork just beyond the church and cross the bridge over the River Allen. Continue to and cross the B3078.

Follow the winding road past the entrance to Gaunt's House and ride on to the junction at Pig Oak. Turn right to Grange. At the crossroads in Grange turn left to Merry Field Hill. Take the third turning on the right, which will pass the Horns Inn, and return down Burts Hill to the junction with the B3078. Turn left and return to Wimborne Minster.

Points of interest

▲ Crichel House: in 1742 the seventeenth-century manor house was burnt down and in 1765 the estate passed to the son of Humphrey Sturt of Horton House. He built the present house and to improve the setting removed the entire village of More Crichel except the church. He then landscaped the whole area as parkland, complete with a large lake. The displaced villagers were rehoused in a new village called Newtown, a mile away in the parish of Witchampton.

The Drover's Inn near Amen Corner, Gussage All Saints

Ride 17
TO THE ROMAN CROSSROADS AT BADBURY RINGS

Distance: 21 miles Journey time: approximately 4 hours

Route Description

The many highlights on this ride include the White Mill Bridge at Sturminster Marshall, the site of the Roman ford at Shapwick, the beautiful Beech Avenue near Kingston Lacy, Badbury Rings, Kingston Lacy House, the village of Pamphill and Wimborne itself. From Wimborne the route goes to Corfe Mullen and Lytchett Matravers through a delightfully wooded area popular with horse and pony enthusiasts. The open countryside beyond Lytchett Matravers is dominated by the extensive woods and land of Charborough Park, whose hidden presence is indicated by the Observation Tower which can be seen rising above the trees.

Sturminster Marshall contains many delightful houses and is particularly noted for its medieval White Mill Bridge across the River Stour, which is never far from this route. The ride follows the course of the river to the village of Shapwick and from there along the Roman road to Badbury Rings, where a tour of the Iron Age hill fort is highly recommended.

The final stage begins with a ride along the remarkable Beech Avenue to the turning to White Mill and from there to Pamphill and Wimborne. The ride through Pamphill makes a delightful end to a rewarding and enjoyable excursion.

Start (OS Landranger sheet 195. Grid reference ST006000.)

Leave the car park in Old Road, Wimborne, and at the T-junction turn right onto Victoria Road. At the small roundabout bear right down Julians Road (the B3073), cross Julians Bridge and at a second roundabout take the road directly ahead, which is signposted to Corfe Mullen (South). Continue to a third roundabout, taking the second exit, a minor road which leads to a junction with the Blandford Road (the B3074), on the outskirts of Corfe Mullen.

Points of interest

▲   Wimborne Minster: an ancient market town on the River Stour; its recorded history dates back to the eighth century. The Minster's main features are the lantern tower, an 800-year-old font and a chained library. Other interesting buildings are the thirteenth-century St Margaret's Hospital chapel and the Priest's House, a sixteenth-century building, now the town's museum.

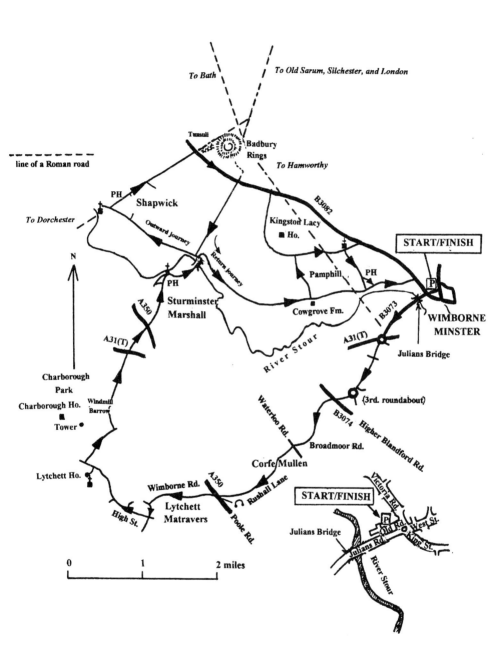

Turn right onto the Blandford Road and then almost immediately left down Pardys Hill, a steep hill leading down Broadmoor Road through an area of pleasant woodland. Pass Brook Lane and Brook Lane Farm on the left. At the crossroads cross Waterloo Road to join Rushall Lane. Follow this lane through attractive woodland to the crossroads at the Poole Road (the A350).

Cross the Poole Road and join the Wimborne Road to Lytchett Matravers. Pass Dowdens Farm on the right, keep straight on and at the fork bear left along Wareham Road. This leads to a junction with High Street. Turn right towards Alma. Ride along High Street and out of the town, passing a concrete water tower on the right.

Continue down Colehill Road past Lytchett House on the left. Take the next right turn along Dullar Lane (signposted on the left-hand side of the road). Follow this narrow road as it rises gently to a fork. Bear left and ride up to Windmill Barrow. Charborough House lies away to the left, hidden by the trees of High Wood. The Observation Tower in Charborough Park can, however, be clearly seen. Continue to the junction with the A31(T).

Go straight across and ride to the Give Way sign at the junction with the A350. Go straight across again and ride along Station Road into Sturminster Marshall. At the mini-roundabout keep straight on down High Street to the Church of St Mary the Virgin in Church Street, opposite The Red Lion Inn.

Continue down Church Street, following the road as it turns sharp right at Church Farm, and then bearing left before crossing the White Mill Bridge over the River Stour. Ignore the first turning on the right to Cowgrove and also the second turning on the right (Piccadilly Lane), which leads to the Badbury Rings. Ride straight ahead to Shapwick along Stewards Lane. At the village cross turn right along High Street with the Archer Inn on the left.

Points of interest

▲ Sturminster Marshall: well known for its beautiful medieval eight-arched bridge. The Mill, which belongs to the National Trust, can be visited.

▲ Shapwick: a small village on the bank of the River Stour. A Roman road forded the river here.

Stage 2: Shapwick–Badbury Rings–White Mill–Cowgrove–Pamphill–Wimborne

The road from Shapwick to Badbury Rings runs along the line of the Roman road from Dorchester. At the junction with the B3082 cross over to the car park and entrance gate to tour the Iron Age hill fort of Badbury Rings. To continue the ride, rejoin the B3082, turn left and ride through the magnificent Beech Avenue in the direction of Wimborne. Take the first turning on the right (after about 0.5 miles) to Sturminster Marshall and White Mill.

Follow this long straight road to a T-junction near the mill. Turn left and left again along the minor road to Cowgrove and Wimborne. The road swings round to the right before straightening out. Take the first turning on the left, up Roman Way, which is opposite Cowgrove Farm. Follow this road towards a wood and turn right at the T-junction near the edge of the wood. Keep on this road as far as St Stephen's Church. Turn right here down the road opposite the church. It runs through an avenue of trees past the old manor house and the village sports field, both of which are on the right.

At Pamphill Green, a triangle of grass, bear left and pass the Vine Inn before descending the steep Vine Hill to a T-junction. Turn left and follow the road to the junction with the B3082. In Wimborne, turn right onto Victoria Road and ride the short distance back to Old Road and the car park.

Points of interest

▲   Badbury Rings: an Iron Age hill fort with Bronze Age burial mounds, deep ditches and high ramparts. According to legend, King Arthur met the Saxons in battle here. Many Roman roads radiate from the hill, among them the London–Exeter road.

▲   The Beech Avenue: this avenue, planted in 1835, is situated on the Blandford to Wimborne road and stretches for 2.5 miles.

▲   Kingston Lacy House: once a royal manor, the present house was built in the seventeenth century by Sir Ralph Bankes, whose home at Corfe Castle was destroyed by Cromwell. The house is set in a lovely eighteenth-century landscaped park and is now in the care of the National Trust.

Kingston Lacy House, near Wimborne Minster

▲ Pamphill: a delightful village which includes the Kingston Lacy estate. It has a rich mixture of houses and a fine avenue of oak trees leading down from the entrance to St Stephen's Church to the village sports field. A Roman road from Badbury Rings crosses through the village to a ford over the River Stour before making its way to Hamworthy.

Ride 18

FROM BERE REGIS TO THE CHALK UPLAND VILLAGES

Distance: 20.5 miles **Journey time:** *approximately 5 hours*

Route Description

The journey begins in the historic village of Bere Regis, which lies on the fringe of the chalk uplands, and heads towards Winterborne Kingston and Winterborne Whitechurch. From there the route turns north-west to Milton Abbas, Hilton and Ansty, villages that lie in the heart of the chalk uplands. The return journey begins in Melcombe Bingham and wends its way down to and crosses the Dewlish Brook. There follows a short climb over a chalk ridge to join the road to Milborne St Andrew, from where the rider can locate the road back to Bere Regis.

This is a moderately easy journey considering the reputation this region has for difficult cycling. The only three short sections which might cause the occasional rider to dismount are, firstly, the short climb from the lakeside at Milton Abbas, secondly, the climb up the valley from the village of Hilton, and finally the short climb from Dewlish Brook. However, they will not detract from the pleasure of a ride which offers so much.

Start *(OS Landranger sheet 194. Grid reference SY844947.)*

Leave the car park in Turberville Court, turn left into Turberville Road and then right at the junction with Manor Farm Road. Turn right into West Street, passing the Drax Arms before turning left down North Street. Although this street is classified as a cul-de-sac there is access for cyclists to the roundabout linking the Bere Regis by-pass and the A31(T). From the roundabout join the A31(T), paying due care and attention to the busy traffic. Ride for approximately 1 mile along the A31 before turning left at the sign to Winterborne Kingston. From the A31 the road rises steadily to a summit at Hey Tor Farm. Ride down into Winterborne Kingston.

Points of interest

▲ Bere Regis: the birthplace of Simon de Montfort, Earl of Leicester (1200–65), founder of the English Parliament. The church is a fifteenth-century building. It has a series of arches supported by columns, known as an arcade, which was built by the Normans. The magnificent timber roof was contributed by John Morton (1420–1500) who was made Archbishop of Canterbury in 1486 and later Lord Chancellor. Members of the Turberville family, relatives of Morton, are buried in the church.

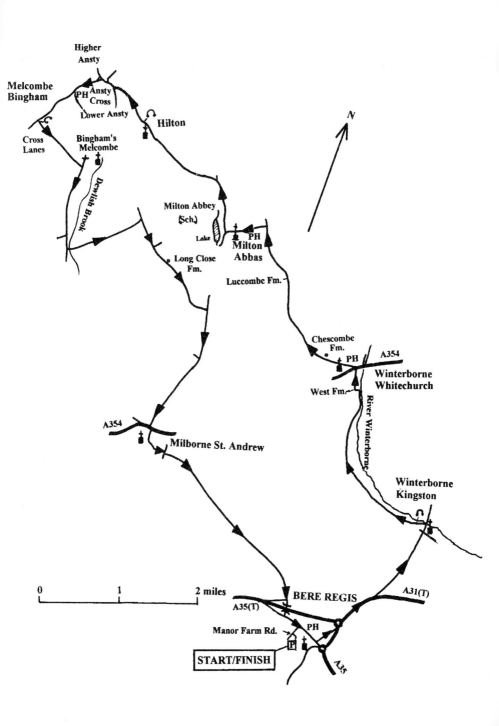

Higher
Ansty

Melcombe
Bingham

PH Ansty
Cross

Lower Ansty

Hilton

Cross
Lanes

Bingham's
Melcombe

Dewlish Brook

Milton Abbey
(Sch.)

Lake

PH
Milton
Abbas

Long Close
Fm.

Luccombe Fm.

Chescombe
Fm.

PH   A354

West Fm.

Winterborne
Whitechurch

River Winterborne

A354

Milborne St. Andrew

Winterborne
Kingston

0   1   2 miles

BERE REGIS

A31(T)

A35(T)

Manor Farm Rd.

PH

P

START/FINISH

A35

N

Stage 1: *Winterborne Kingston–Winterborne Whitechurch–Milton Abbas*

In Winterborne Kingston turn left by the war memorial into West Street and the road to Winterborne Whitechurch. The road rises gently before flattening out and passing East Farm on the right. The road then turns sharp left and then sharp right by West Farm before reaching the junction with the A354 in Winterborne Whitechurch. Go straight across this road to join the road to Milton Abbas. This passes the Milton Arms and the Church of St Mary before leaving the village. The road rises steadily, passing Chescombe Farm on the right and, further on, Luccombe Farm, a business and craft centre. Continue along this road, turning left at the sign to Milton Abbas. The road runs down through the village, passing the Hambro Arms before arriving at the lake. Turn right here for Hilton.

Points of interest
▲ Winterborne Whitechurch: birthplace of John Wesley's father.
▲ Milton Abbas: Joseph Damer acquired the estate of Milton Abbas in 1752 and built the present mansion beside the abbey church. To obtain privacy he demolished the village properties which were too close to his mansion and relocated and rebuilt the houses, almshouses, the school and church on the present site in Milton Abbas.

Stage 2: *Milton Abbas–Hilton–Ansty–Melcombe Bingham–Bingham's Melcombe–Milborne St Anrew–Bere Regis*

Pass Lake Lodge and make the short but steep climb to a wooded area overlooking the Milton Abbas School. Follow the road as it drops down to and through a tunnel, passing the rear of the school before sweeping left round by the sportsfields and continuing to Hilton. It is at this section of the journey that the best view of the school and its environment can be enjoyed.

The road then swings to the right up the valley before proceeding to drop in a series of steps into the village of Hilton. Ride through the village, passing the church on the left, before beginning the climb out of the valley towards Ansty Cross. Turn right at the T-junction at the top of the climb. Disregard the turn on the right to Bulbarrow and continue directly ahead to Ansty. At the building at the triangle of land (Ansty Cross) bear left into Lower Ansty and then on towards Melcombe Bingham. The route passes the Fox Inn on the left before crossing a stream and climbing up into Melcombe Bingham. Ride through the village to the signpost at Cross Lanes, near the telephone box.

Turn left to Bingham's Melcombe and Dewlish. This narrow lane passes between high banks to the gates at the entrance to Bingham's Melcombe, a country house of character. Although there is a No Access sign, members of the public are allowed to visit the church, which can be reached via the main driveway.

Continue the journey from Bingham's Melcombe and follow the narrow lane as it runs along the side of the valley. Disregard the next turning on the right and continue straight on in the direction of Dewlish and Milton Abbas. At the next junction turn left towards Milton Abbas, cross the Dewlish Brook and climb up the narrow road to a T-junction. Turn right towards Milborne St Andrew and Milton Abbas. Pass the Rare Pig and Poultry Centre on the left. Ignore any turnings on the left to Milton Abbas and ride straight ahead to a Give Way sign at a T-junction. Turn right to Milborne St Andrew (2 miles).

Turn left at the junction with the A354 in Milborne St Andrew and then first right down a narrow lane almost directly opposite the post office. This leads to and rises up through a housing estate to a Give Way sign. Go straight aross to join the road signposted to Bere Regis. Follow it as it drops down to the bridge over the A35(T). Pass under the bridge and bear left to join the main street in Bere Regis and return to the car park.

Points of interest

▲ Milborne St Andrew: birthplace of John Morton, Archbishop of Canterbury in 1486 and Lord Chancellor in 1487 during the reign of Henry VII.

The white marble memorial to Sir Joseph Damer's wife by Carlini (1775), Milton Abbey

Ride 19

BRIDPORT TO ABBOTSBURY

Distance: 26.5 miles Journey time: approximately 4 hours

Route Description

The tour begins in the market town of Bridport and heads to the village of Bradpole, north of the town. From here the ride follows the Askers Brook to Loders, a charming village hidden in a deep narrow valley, and Uploders, a village lying in the shadow of the great earthwork of Eggardon Hill. Askerswell is the last of these villages and it is from here that the ride climbs Askerswell Down to the A35(T) before dropping into the valley of the River Bride.

The route zigzags its way above the river through Litton Cheney, Long Bredy and Littlebredy before climbing out of the valley and heading towards Black Down. The solitude of the valley and the attractiveness of the villages make this a most interesting cycling area.

A minor road on the slopes of Black Down provides an exciting, freewheeling run down to Abbotsbury, where the return journey to Bridport begins with a climb up the coast road (B3157) to the summit near the hill fort of Abbotsbury Castle. Although it is a long climb, it is gradual, and ends with magnificent views of Chesil Beach, the sea and coastline. In addition, on the return run along the coast road through Swyre and Burton Bradstock the ever-changing coastal scene can be appreciated.

This is a route more suited to the experienced rider and not to younger members of the family. However, as with all the rides in this book, selected sections away from the main roads can be used and thoroughly enjoyed. In this case a ride beginning in Bradpole and following the Askers Brook through Loders, Uploders and Askerswell would provide a short but pleasant alternative ride.

Start (OS Landranger sheets 193 and 194. Grid reference for sheet 193: ST462927.)
The ride begins in Bridport, from the car park near the river bridge in West Street. Leave the car park, turn right into West Street and ride straight on past the building with the clock tower into East Street. Continue down East Street and at the roundabout take the second exit, East Road. This is the A35(T) Bridport–Dorchester road. Ride along East Road to where a small traffic island stands in the centre of the road and turn left along Lee Lane. There is a telephone box at the entrance to this narrow lane. Follow Lee Lane as it passes into open countryside before sweeping down and round a sharp left-hand bend to a bridge over the Mangerton River.

Points of interest

▲ Bridport: a market town on the River Brit. It has long been a manufacturing centre for twine, netting, sail-cloth and rope, and its extra-wide pavements were constructed on

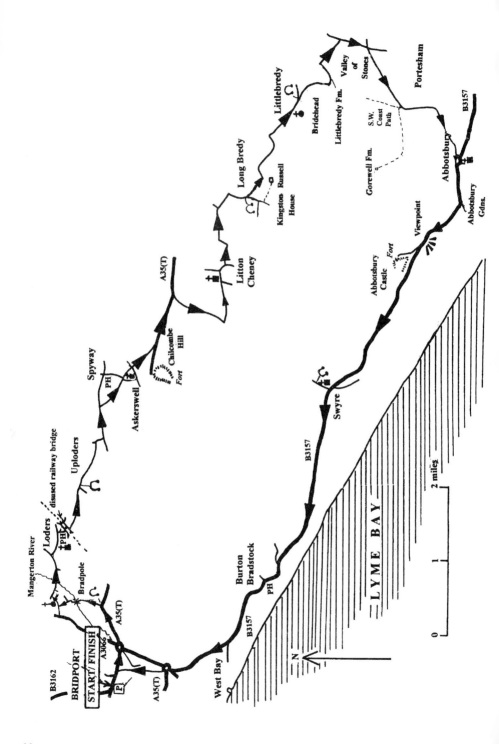

90

that scale to make rope 'walks' for drying twine. Bridport is a good centre for exploring West Dorset.

Stage 1: Bradpole–Loders–Uploders–Askerswell–Litton Cheney

From the bridge over the Mangerton River in Bradpole follow the road as it bears right and then left across an unused railway crossing. Ride straight ahead along Trinity Way to a T-junction. Turn right to Loders (1 mile) and Askerswell (3 miles). Pass Court House and the church on the left and at the fork bear left to a T-junction. Turn right to Loders. Ignore the road to the right and pass across the river bridge. Pass Loders Mill on the right and carry straight on into Loders. Ride through the village and follow the road under a disused railway bridge. Cross the bridge over the stream and bear left with the road as it passes Higher Yondover Farm.

The road to Uploders gives excellent views of the hill fort on Eggardon Hill away to the left. Ride through the village and follow the road as it turns sharp right and then left as it heads towards Askerswell. At the next fork bear right to Askerswell. The road rises and then drops down to a crossroads in the centre of the village. Go straight across and follow the road out of the village to another crossroads. Go straight across again to join the road marked with a gradient sign of 17 per cent. This runs up the side of Chilcombe Hill and leads to the A35(T).

At the Give Way sign turn left onto the A35 and take the first turning on the right to Litton Cheney. The turning is situated opposite the gate to Stancombe Farm. Please note that the A35 is a busy road and it is recommended that cyclists dismount and cross this carriageway on foot. This road twists its way down to a sharp bend before making its final descent to a road junction in the village. Bear left and keep straight on. At the next junction bear right and ride through the village. Keep to the left at the fork where a sign on the nearby wall reads 'Litton Cheney'. Carry straight on, with Glebe Cottage to the right.

Points of interest

▲ Bradpole: lies on a chalk stream known as the Mangerton River. On the churchyard wall is a memorial plaque to W.E. Forster, the minister responsible for Education Act of 1870 which saw the start of Board schools and the beginning of general schooling for the mass of working people.

▲ Loders: a village hidden in a deep valley with Waddon Hill at one end, Boars Barrow at the other and the Askers Brook flowing through it. The Benedictines founded a priory here in 1100; it was dissolved by Henry V, who refused to pay dues to the mother house in France. The church has a curious small room over the porch where an English priest appointed by the monks to care for the villagers used to lodge.

Stage 2: Litton Cheney–Long Bredy–Littlebredy–Abbotsbury

The road from Litton Cheney passes Dowerfield Farm and drops down through a wood, turning sharply to the right near a large house on the left before reaching a fork in the centre of Long Bredy. Bear left here to Littlebredy. To catch a glimpse of Kingston Russell House in its attractive setting, bear right at this fork, disregard the next road on the right and travel the short distance down the road, signposted as a cul-de-sac as far as the gates leading to the house. The house is privately owned and not open to the public. This is a short diversion and well worth while. Return to the fork to continue to Littlebredy.

The road rises from the fork in Long Bredy with views of Kingston Russell House before bearing sharp left and then right up to Watcombe Farm, high above the valley. The twisting and turning continues before straightening on the approach to the gatehouse at the entrance to Littlebredy. Pass the church, bear right at the fork and follow the road as it sweeps to the right, passing the cricket ground at Bridehead. There follows a climb to Littlebredy Farm and a further climb to a T-junction high above the valley. Turn right at this junction and at the next T-junction turn right again towards Portesham.

Follow the road down to a crossroads and turn right. This is signposted to Gorwell Farm but also leads down to Abbotsbury. The road runs down towards the entrance to Gorewell Farm, where it turns sharp left before running into Abbotsbury. Bear right at the fork in the village, where there are tearooms and public toilets.

Points of interest
▲   Long Bredy: Kingston Russell House was the birthplace (in 1769) of Captain Thomas Masterman Hardy, who served under Admiral Nelson.
▲   Littlebredy: a delightful village sheltered by the downs. Near Littlebredy Farm is a

Swans at Abbotsbury

valley known as the Valley of the Stones which is strewn with sarsens (boulders carried by ice during the Ice Ages) and dolmens (megalithic tombs with a large flat stone laid on upright ones). A footpath near the farm leads to this valley.

▲ Abbotsbury: a very old and attractive village lying in a sheltered valley near the Chesil Bank, Abbotsbury has much to offer the visitor. The gatehouse and large tithe barn of its eleventh-century Benedictine abbey remain, while on a nearby hill stands the fifteenth-century St Catherine's Chapel. Down on the shore of the lagoon known as West Fleet is the 600-year-old swannery. Another attraction is the sub-tropical gardens.

Stage 3: Abbotsbury–Swyre–Burton Bradstock–West Bay–Bridport

There is a long climb on the B3157 out of Abbotsbury to the hill fort of Abbotsbury Castle. From the roadside vantage point here there is a magnificent view over the Chesil Beach and the coastline towards Burton Bradstock. The ride to Swyre and Burton Bradstock follows the coast and offers an opportunity of visiting West Bay, the small port near Bridport. From Burton Bradstock the B3157 leads to a roundabout at Bothenhampton on the outskirts of Bridport. Take the third exit, which will bring you along South Street to the traffic lights next to the clock tower in the centre of the town. Go straight ahead at the lights, then turn left along West Street to the car park.

Points of interest
▲ Burton Bradstock: the famous Chesil Beach begins here and extends eastwards to Portland.

Ride 20

IN THE WAKE OF THOMAS HARDY
AND LAWRENCE OF ARABIA

Distance: 24 miles Journey time: 3–4 hours

Route Description

This is an easy ride along the valley of the River Frome, full of variety, and there are opportunities to visit many places of interest. The lovely Dorset villages of this region, like West Stafford, Woodsford and Moreton, made an early and enduring impression on Thomas Hardy. T.E. Lawrence worked at Bovington Camp and Clouds Hill was his last home. The Atomic Energy Establishment at East Burton is a sharp reminder of the present, but the return journey to Dorchester runs through Pallington and Tincleton, where the tranquil landscape remains relatively unchanged.

Start *(OS Landranger sheet 194. Grid reference SY696906.)*

Leave the central public car park in Dorchester and turn right into Acland Road. At the T-junction turn left into The South Walks Road and at the mini-roundabout turn left along Icen Way. Continue along this road to the junction with High East Street (the B3150), the main road through the town. Turn right down London Road, the extension to High East Street, cross over the River Frome at Greys Bridge and continue up to the roundabout at the top of Stinsford Hill. Join the roundabout and leave at the exit to Stinsford. Pass the entrance to the Dorset College of Agriculture and continue to a crossroads.

Points of interest

▲ Dorchester: the Durnovaria of the Romans, who founded it in about AD 70. The Maumbury Rings, formerly a neolithic henge monument, became a Roman amphitheatre; they can be visited. In the Dorset County Museum are displayed a collection of archaeological material and Roman artefacts from many parts of the county. Thomas Hardy, the poet and novelist, and William Barnes, the Dorsetshire poet, both have strong associations with the town and Hardy's study is preserved in the museum. Judge Jeffreys lodged in what is now the Lodging Restaurant in High West Street during the Bloody Assizes of 1685. Across the road is the old Shire Hall, where the trial of the Tolpuddle Martyrs was held. The courtroom is open to the public.

Stage 1: Stinsford–Higher Bockhampton–Lower Bockhampton–
         West Stafford–Woodsford

Turn left at the crossroads to visit Thomas Hardy's Cottage at Higher Bockhampton and

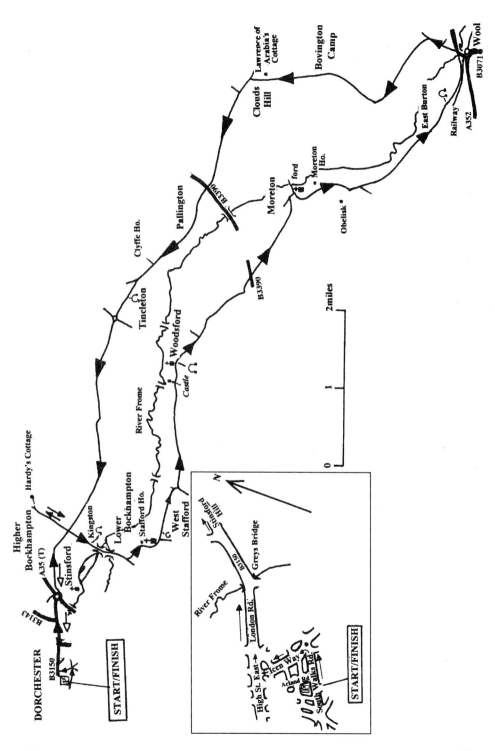

95

afterwards return to it to continue the journey. From the crossroads follow the signposted direction to Lower Bockhampton and West Stafford. Pass through the small hamlet of Lower Bockhampton with Thomas Hardy's first school on the right before crossing the little hump-backed bridge over the River Frome. To visit Stinsford church follow the riverside path on the right at the far side of the bridge. This was one of Hardy's favourite walks.

After the bridge take the next turn on the left to West Stafford (0.5 miles) and Woodsford (3.5 miles). Pass the entrance to Stafford House on the left and follow the road as it bears left by the church. Keep straight on through the village and beyond to the next T-junction. Turn left to Woodsford and follow the road past Woodsford Castle, bearing right by the telephone box.

Points of interest

▲   Higher Bockhampton: a tiny hamlet with an old thatched cottage, the birthplace of Thomas Hardy and now a National Trust property, on the edge of Puddletown Heath (the

Hardy's Cottage, Higher Bockhampton

'Egdon Heath' of Hardy's *The Return of the Native*). He also wrote *Under the Greenwood Tree* and *Far from the Madding Crowd* here. His heart is buried with his first wife in the churchyard at Stinsford near by.

▲ Lower Bockhampton: Hardy's first school stands near the bridge over the river, and his family's graves lie in the grounds of Stinsford church.

▲ Woodsford Castle: originally built as a fortified manor house during the reign of Edward III (1312–77), it was later converted into a farmhouse.

Stage 2: Woodsford–Moreton–East Burton–Wool–Bovington Camp

Continue along this road past the entrance to Woodsford Lower Dairy Farm and on through a wood to a crossroads at the B3390. Go straight across and ride down this long tree-lined road into Moreton, a village worthy of exploration.

From Moreton follow the signposted road to East Burton and Wool. To the left stands Moreton House, and a memorial obelisk to one of the members of the Frampton family rises above the trees on a hill to the right just beyond the village. On the approach to East Burton the Winfrith Atomic Energy Establishment buildings can be seen on the right on the opposite side of the railway line. Follow the road past the Seven Stars public house to the junction with the A352. The Wool railway station and signal box are situated on the right. Turn left onto the A352 and take the first turning on the left. Cross the bridge over the River Frome, pass Woolbridge Manor Farm and continue past the first road on the right. Turn left at the next fork. Follow the road through Bovington Camp to Clouds Hill, the former home of T.E. Lawrence, which stands on the right a short distance from a T-junction.

Points of interest

▲ Moreton: a small village on the River Frome whose cemetery contains the grave of Lawrence of Arabia. St Nicholas' Church, which is separate from the cemetery, has remarkable engraved chancel windows. It was Squire Frampton of Moreton House who played a prominent part in the prosecution of the Tolpuddle Martyrs. The high obelisk to the southeast commemorates James Frampton.

▲ Wool: the sixteenth-century Woolbridge and Woolbridge Manor feature in Thomas Hardy's *Tess of the D'Urbervilles*. The house once belonged to the Dorset family of Turberville.

▲ Bovington Camp: the Tank Museum here has a large and comprehensive collection of armoured fighting vehicles. It is open all the year round except Christmas and New Year.

▲ Clouds Hill: the home of Lawrence of Arabia at the time of his fatal accident. A National Trust property, it is open to the public.

Stage 3: Clouds Hill–Pallington–Tincleton–Dorchester

Turn left at the T-junction just beyond Clouds Hill and follow the road to the crossroads at the B3390. Go straight across and pass through Pallington. Bear left at the fork and continue straight ahead at the crossroads in Tincleton. The road will eventually arrive back at the Bockhampton crossroads. Follow the route from here back to the roundabout and Dorchester.

Woodsford Castle

Ride 21

ACROSS THE UPLANDS TO THE VALLEYS OF THE FROME AND SYDLING WATER

Distance: 24 miles Journey time: 5–6 hours

Route Description

Reminders of the prehistoric and Roman occupation of this part of Dorset are ever present in a journey that leaves Dorchester for the expanse of the chalk ridge overlooking the valley of the River Frome. This upland area, which appears devoid of human habitation, is tended from the farms that lie below the ridge. Usually sited near spring water that emerges from the chalk, they can be seen on the downhill run to Wynford Eagle.

From Maiden Newton there is a long hill climb to join the Yeovil to Dorchester road briefly before descending into the valley of the Sydling Water and the charming village of Sydling St Nicholas. The abundant strip lynchets, the tumuli and the well-defined outline of an early settlement on Grimstone Down make this an exceptional valley. It ends where it meets the Yeovil to Dorchester road and the Sydling Water joins the River Frome at Grimstone.

From Muckleford, a short distance away, tranquillity returns for the journey to Bradford Peverell and Dorchester. The final stretch of the ride beyond Bradford Peverell is in an area where there are many tumuli and long barrows. In addition there is a clearly defined outline of the Roman aqueduct and the prominent fortifications of Poundbury hill fort.

This is a ride which is recommended for experienced cyclists and not for young children.

Start (OS Landranger sheet 194. Grid reference SY693903.)

Leave the central public car park in Dorchester and turn right into Acland Road. Turn right at the T-junction into The South Walks Road. Pass through the traffic lights and go straight across to join the road called Great Western. Ride straight ahead at the next crossroads to join Damers Road. Pass under a railway bridge and at the junction with the Bridport Road bear left along this straight Roman Road towards a roundabout. Go straight ahead at the roundabout following the A35(T) towards Honiton.

Approximately 2 miles from the roundabout the road curves to the right before swinging left and down a steep hill. The minor road across the uplands is on the right near the bottom of this hill. Because of the awkwardness of the bend in the A35 at this point it is advisable to dismount and walk across to join the minor road.

Points of interest

▲ Dorchester: the Durnovaria of the Romans, who founded the town in about AD 70. The Maumbury Rings, formerly a neolithic henge monument, became a Roman amphitheatre;

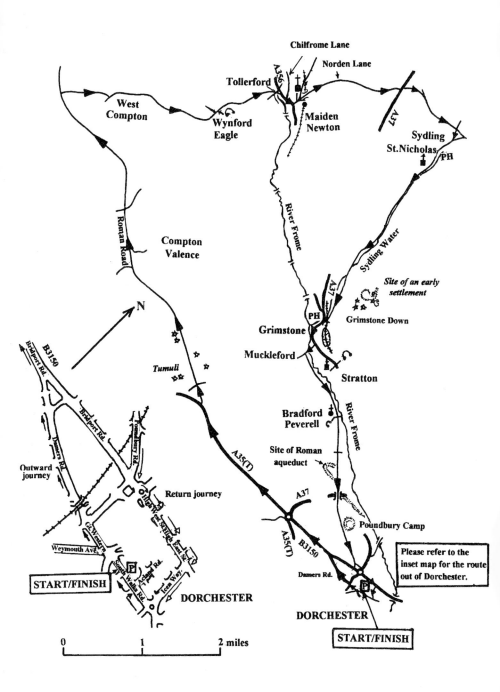

Chilfrome Lane

Norden Lane

Tollerford

West Compton

Wynford Eagle

Maiden Newton

Sydling St.Nicholas
PH

Roman Road

Compton Valence

River Frome

Sydling Water

Site of an early settlement

N

Grimstone Down

PH

Grimstone

Muckleford

Stratton

B3150

Bridport Rd.

Tumuli

Bridport Rd.

Poundbury Rd.

Damers Rd.

Bradford Peverell

River Frome

Outward journey

Return journey

A35(T)

Site of Roman aqueduct

A37

High West St.
East St.

A35(T)

B3150

Poundbury Camp

Please refer to the inset map for the route out of Dorchester.

G. Wester..

Weymouth Ave.

South Walks Rd.

Acland Rd.

Icen Way

Damers Rd.

P

P

START/FINISH

DORCHESTER

DORCHESTER

START/FINISH

0   1   2 miles

they can be visited. Thomas Hardy, the poet and novelist, and William Barnes, the Dorsetshire poet, have strong associations with the town and Hardy's study is preserved in the County Museum. Judge Jeffreys lodged in what is now the Lodging Restaurant in High West Street in Dorchester during the Bloody Assizes of 1685. Across the road is the old Shire Hall, where the trial of the Tolpuddle Martyrs was held. The courtroom is open to the public.

Stage 1: A35(T)–West Compton–Wynford Eagle–Tollerford–Maiden Newton

Follow the minor road and ride straight ahead at the crossroads. Pass the entrance roads to Townhill Farm and Hogleaze Farm on the right and disregard the turning to Compton Valence.

At the next crossroads ride straight ahead towards Eggardon Hill and Askerswell. Take the next right turn to West Compton, Wynford Eagle and Maiden Newton. The road runs downhill to Wynford Eagle. From here the road rises gently before continuing to a T-junction in Tollerford.

Turn left, cross the bridge over the River Frome and bear right to the junction with the A356. Turn right onto the A356, pass the road to Chilfrome on the left and cross over the river. Pass the Castle Inn on the right, cross another bridge and ride to the town cross in Maiden Newton.

Points of interest

▲ Wynford Eagle: a small hamlet with an attractive seventeenth-century manor house which has a large stone eagle perched on the central gable. This was once the home of the Sydenham family. Dr Thomas Sydenham (1624–89), who is regarded as the father of English medicine, was born at Wynford Eagle and was one of five brothers who fought for Parliament during the Civil War. He was the first physician carefully to observe the symptoms of a disease in order to arrive at a correct diagnosis. He was sceptical about the value of bleeding and used quinine in the treatment of malaria.

▲ Maiden Newton: an historic town with traces of both early British and Roman settlements. At the rear of the fifteenth-century Church of St Mary there is a door with bullet holes made by the guns of Cromwell's soldiers. The door still hangs on its original hinges and is protected by a glass frame.

Stage 2: Maiden Newton–Sydling St Nicholas–Muckleford–Bradford Peverell
–Dorchester

From the town cross in Maiden Newton turn left down Church Road and bear right along Norden Lane at the war memorial. Within a short distance the road appears to split into three. The road to the right leads to the railway station, the one to the left is the Cattistock road and the one in the centre is Norden Lane. Follow Norden Lane. This road climbs to and crosses the railway bridge and continues climbing a further 1.5 miles before levelling out to meet the A37.

Turn left onto the A37 and then almost immediately right to Sydling St Nicholas. Ride down to the crossroads in the valley bottom and turn right. Cycle into Sydling St Nicholas, passing the Pound Inn on the left. Continue by keeping to the main road which runs alongside Sydling Water. Pass Magiston Farm on the left, ignore the turning on the right to Frampton and cross the bridge over Sydling Water. Away to the left across the fields can be seen the remarkably clear outline of an early settlement and tumuli on Grimstone Down. Pass under the railway bridge to the junction with the A37. Turn left, pass the Royal Yeoman Inn in Grimstone and take the next turning on the right to Muckleford.

Cross the bridge over the River Frome and turn left. Follow this road alongside the river to Bradford Peverell. Pass through the village and keep straight on at the crossroads. From here there is a steep climb to a stretch of Roman road from which the curving grass mounds of the Roman aqueduct can be identified in the field on the right just beyond a wood.

Cross the bridge over the A37, pass Poundbury Camp on the left and ride to the junction with Bridport Road. Turn left and keep straight ahead at the roundabout down High West Street and its continuation, High East Street, to the second right turn (Icen Way). Ride along Icen Way and at the mini-roundabout turn right along South Walks Road to the car park.

Points of interest

▲ Sydling St Nicholas: this is a picturesque village with some interesting houses. The fifteenth-century church has a fireplace in the porch where parish meetings were once

A quiet corner of Sydling St Nicholas

held. The church has one of the oldest clocks in England, dating from 1593. It is faceless but strikes the hours. Beside the church is the manor house, which once belonged to Elizabeth I's favourite, Sir Francis Walsingham.

▲ Bradford Peverell: noted as the birthplace of John Hutchins, the famous Dorset historian. One of its rectors, Dr Howley, became Archbishop of Canterbury and crowned Queen Victoria. The Roman aqueduct was built to bring water to the West Gate at Dorchester. Most of the large Roman houses in the town were connected by a wooden mains supply, and an open channel can still be seen at Fordington Bottom, north-west of Dorchester.

▲ Poundbury Camp: an Iron-age hill fort close to Dorchester. Excavations of the nearby area have revealed evidence of a thousand Christian burials in the fourth century.

Ride 22

FROM DORCHESTER TO BLACK DOWN AND THE SEA

Distance: 26 miles Journey time: 5–6 hours

Route Description

There are reminders of two famous sons of Dorset on this ride, which goes through a landscape steeped in history. The tour begins in Dorchester (the Roman Durnovaria and a town which was a source of inspiration to Thomas Hardy) and travels alongside the defensive ditches of Maiden Castle on its way to Martinstown and on to the memorial to Sir Thomas Masterman Hardy, Nelson's flagship captain at Trafalgar. Set high on Black Down among ancient barrows and earthworks, the memorial commands wide views over the surrounding land and the sea.

From the memorial the road runs down Portesham Hill into Portesham, where the route follows a by-road tucked beneath the downs through the hamlets of Waddon, Coryates and Friar Waddon and on to the sea at Weymouth. From Weymouth the ride runs along the sea front, moving inland to Overcombe and Preston before joining the road to Sutton Poyntz. On the final ascent to Green Hill and Came Wood before the return to Dorchester there are wonderful views over Weymouth Bay.

The climbs from Martinstown to the Hardy Monument and from Sutton Poyntz to Green Hill and Came Wood should not deter any cyclist from making such a memorable journey.

Start (OS Landranger 194. Grid reference SY693903.)

Leave the central public car park in Dorchester and turn right into Acland Road. At the T-junction turn right into The South Walks Road. Ride straight across at the traffic lights and take the second left (Weymouth Avenue). Pass the Maumbury Ring on the left and at the crossroads continue straight ahead over the railway bridge to join the B3147 Weymouth Road.

Points of interest

▲ Dorchester: the Durnovaria of the Romans, founded in about AD 70. The Maumbury Rings, formerly a neolithic henge monument, became a Roman amphitheatre; they can be visited. Thomas Hardy, the poet and novelist, and William Barnes, the Dorsetshire poet, have strong associations with the town and Hardy's study is preserved in the County Museum. Judge Jeffreys lodged in what is now the Lodge Restaurant in High West Street during the Bloody Assizes of 1685. Across the road is the old Shire Hall, where the trial of the Tolpuddle Martyrs was held. The courtroom is open to the public.

Continue along the Weymouth Road and turn right at the signpost to Winterborne Monkton. Follow the road until you see a gated unclassified road on the right, just before the village. Pass through the gateway and proceed along this narrow but well-surfaced road as it rises before passing near the defensive ditches of the hill fort of Maiden Castle. Cross a stream and at the signposted fork near Ashton Farm bear right to Martinstown.

Within a short distance the road meets the B3159. Turn right and continue to Martinstown. Go past the church and the Brewer's Arms Inn in the village and where the B3159 makes a sharp right turn take the minor road to the left; it leads to the Hardy Monument and Portesham. Climb the hill to the ridge and continue to the monument; here there are panoramic views along the Dorset coastline. From the monument the road runs downhill to a crossroads. Turn left and follow the road as it drops steeply into the village of Portesham.

Points of interest

▲ Maiden Castle: an Iron Age hill fort, the largest in the country, it was captured by the Romans in AD 44.

▲ The Hardy Monument: set 770 feet above sea-level high on Black Down, with wonderful views over the English Channel, the monument was built in 1842 in honour of Sir Thomas Masterman Hardy, Nelson's flag captain at the Battle of Trafalgar.

In Portesham, turn left near the church along a minor road called Winters Lane towards Waddon and Coryates. This road rises before levelling out and making its way beneath the high downs to Waddon and Waddon House. There are excellent views over the Dorset coastline on this gently undulating part of the route.

At the next T-junction bear left towards Friar Waddon and Upwey. (The village of Coryates is to the right at this junction.) The road continues past Corton Farm on the right and through the hamlet of Friar Waddon to a T-junction with the B3159. Turn right and follow the road through Upwey. Where the road bears sharp left near the entrance to Upwey Manor take the minor road on the right which runs by the entrance to the manor. This leads to the village of Broadwey. Pass through the village before bearing left uphill to a T-junction. Turn right and join the A354 Dorchester to Weymouth road.

Points of interest

▲ Portesham: a charming Dorset village with a seveneenth-century manor house (the home of Sir Thomas Masterman Hardy), a medieval church and lovely old stone cottages.

▲ Waddon Manor: a beautiful eighteenth-century manor house.

▲ Upwey: long associated with a wishing-well from which George III is reputed to have drunk, using a golden cup which later became the Ascot Gold Cup. There is also a fine fifteenth-century church and a fine manor house and mill here.

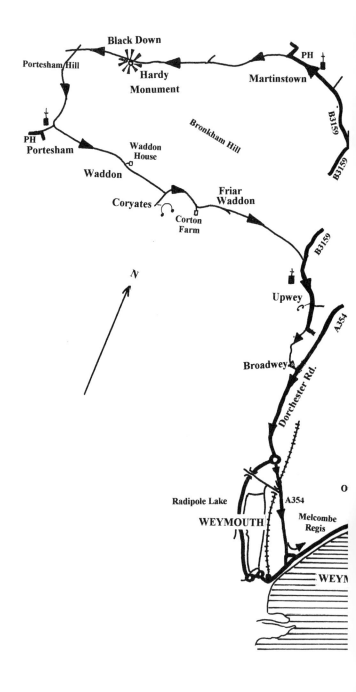

Black Down

Portesham Hill

Hardy
Monument

PH

Martinstown

B3159

B3159

PH
Portesham

Waddon
House

Bronkham Hill

Waddon

Coryates

Corton
Farm

Friar
Waddon

B3159

N

Upwey

A354

Broadwey

Dorchester Rd.

O

Radipole Lake

A354

WEYMOUTH

Melcombe
Regis

WEY

WEYM

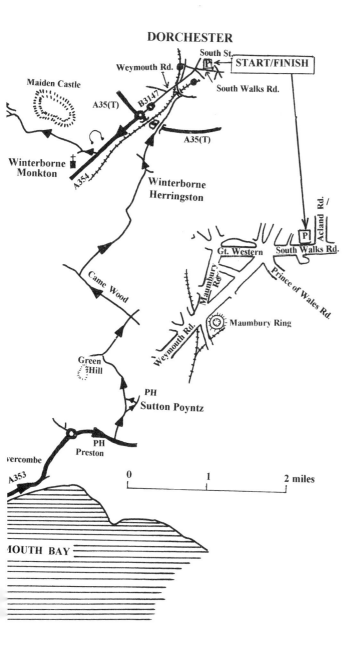

DORCHESTER

South St.

START/FINISH

Weymouth Rd.

South Walks Rd.

Maiden Castle

A35(T)

B3147

Winterborne Monkton

A354

A35(T)

Winterborne Herringston

Acland Rd.

Gt. Western

South Walks Rd.

Came Wood

Maumbury Rd.

Prince of Wales Rd.

Weymouth Rd.

Maumbury Ring

Green Hill

PH
Sutton Poyntz

PH
Preston

vercombe

A353

0   1   2 miles

MOUTH BAY

Waddon House

Stage 3: Weymouth–Preston–Sutton Poyntz–Dorchester

Continue along the A354 and pass through four sets of traffic lights to a roundabout. Bear left along the Dorchester Road. Pass the supermarket on the left, follow the road across the railway bridge and ride straight ahead towards the sea front. Where the road forks, turn left along Westerhall Road. At the Give Way sign turn left along the A353 Preston Road. (Turn right at this fork to visit the town centre. To continue the journey, return along the sea front to rejoin the A353 Preston Road.)

Use the cycle path beside the A353 Preston Road until it ends where the A353 bears sharp left inland. Rejoin the main road and at a roundabout continue on the A353 towards Osmington. Turn left along Sutton Road, near the Spice Ship Inn. This road leads to the village of Sutton Poyntz. At the fork bear right to a delightful corner of the village and the inn.

From the inn take the first left (at the head of the duck pond) and follow this narrow lane to a T-junction. Turn right onto the Dorchester road and climb to the top of Green Hill. Here there are spectacular views over Weymouth. At the T-junction turn right and continue to the crossroads near Came Wood. Turn left, cycle alongside the wood and take the next turning on the right. The road runs downhill by a golf course to an S-bend near Herringston Farm and from there continues through Winterborne Herringston and along Herriston Road into Dorchester.

Turn left along Maumbury Road and at the crossroads turn right down Weymouth Avenue to the car park near The South Walks.

Points of interest
▲ Weymouth: this lovely seaside resort was patronized by George III; it has a busy harbour and quayside, a splendid bay and sandy beaches.
▲ Sutton Poyntz: delightful village straddling a willow-fringed stream. The ancient hill fort of Chalbury is near by.

Ride 23

THROUGH THE PUDDLES
AND THE PIDDLES

Distance: 32 miles (long route), 28 miles (shorter route)
Journey time: 6–7 hours (long route), 5–6 hours (shorter route)

Route Description

This ride begins in Dorchester and heads towards Higher Bockhampton, Puddletown Forest and Puddletown, an area which influenced and inspired the novels of Thomas Hardy. The second part of the journey is from Athelhampton to Tolpuddle and through the tranquil villages on the banks of the River Piddle to Bere Regis, on the edge of the heathland. From here the ride climbs to the chalk uplands, passing through Milborne St Andrew and an area of steep-sided valleys between rolling plateaux to Dewlish and Cheselbourne before dropping down to Piddletrenthide. Piddlehinton is the last of the 'Puddle and Piddle' villages before the return to Dorchester. (The names 'Piddle' and 'Puddle' come from the Old English for 'marsh' or 'fen'.)

The journey may be shortened by turning left at the crossroads below Dewlish and following the route to Higher Waterston and back to Dorchester. Both routes pass through wonderful countryside and the striking contrast between the houses and farms in the river valleys and the almost unpopulated rolling uplands will be appreciated. These routes are hilly and therefore better suited to the regular rider.

It is advisable to take food and drink, as the opportunities for refreshment on this ride are very limited.

Start (OS Landranger 194. Grid reference SY693903.)

Leave the central public car park in Dorchester and turn right into Acland Road. At the T-junction turn left into The South Walks Road and at the mini-roundabout turn left along Icen Way. At the junction with High East Street (B3150), the main road through the town, turn right. Cross the River Frome at Greys Bridge, continue up to the roundabout at the top of Stinsford Hill, and take the exit to Stinsford. Proceed past the entrance to the Dorset College of Agriculture to a crossroads; here, turn left.

Points of interest

▲ Dorchester: the Durnovaria of the Romans, founded in about AD 70. The Maumbury Rings, formerly a neolithic henge monument, became a Roman amphitheatre; they can be visited. Thomas Hardy, the poet and novelist, and William Barnes, the Dorsetshire poet, have strong associations with the town and Hardy's study is preserved in the County Museum. (Hardy's cottage can be seen on this ride.) Judge Jeffreys lodged in what is now the Lodging Restaurant in High West Street during the Bloody Assizes of 1685. Across the road is the old Shire Hall, where the trial of the Tolpuddle Martyrs was held. The court-room is open to the public.

Stage 1: Higher Bockhampton–Puddletown–Tolpuddle

Pass the lane on the right leading to Thomas Hardy's Cottage at Higher Bockhampton (or make a detour if you wish to visit the cottage), and follow the road as it leads to a bridge over the A35(T). Cross the bridge and follow the minor road as it rises gradually through part of Puddletown Forest. The route passes Troy Town Farm before bearing right under the A35(T). Take the first turning on the right after the underpass. The road rises and re-enters the forest. At the fork bear left to Puddletown.

On entering Puddletown continue down New Street to the junction with the A35(T) and turn right. (Alternatively, to visit the church and the centre of Puddletown, cross the A35(T), ride down the lane directly opposite and at the T-junction turn left and follow the road; afterwards, return to the main road and turn left.) Proceed to Tolpuddle (1.75 miles), passing the entrance to the medieval manor at Athelhampton. Pass the Museum to the Tolpuddle Martyrs on the left and take the first turning on the right down The Green past the famous sycamore known as the Martyr's Tree. This road leads to Affpuddle.

Interior of St Mary's Church, Puddletown

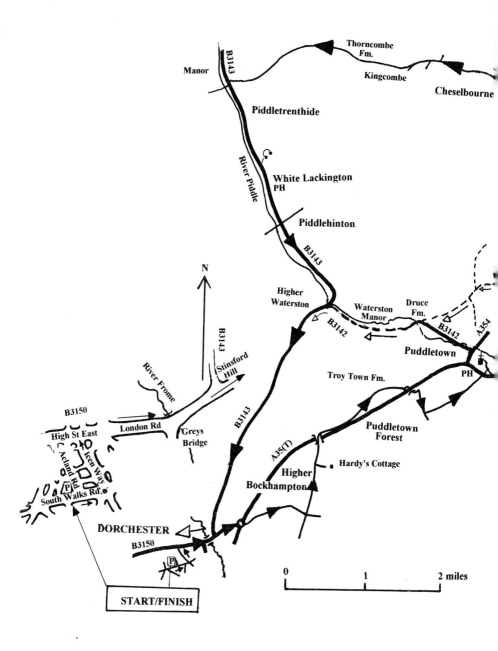

Thorncombe Fm.

Manor

B3143

Kingcombe

Cheselbourne

Piddletrenthide

River Piddle

White Lackington PH

Piddlehinton

B3143

N

Higher Waterston

Waterston Manor

Druce Fm.

B3142

B3142

A354

B3143

Stinsford Hill

Puddletown

PH

River Frome

Troy Town Fm.

B3150

London Rd

High St East

Greys Bridge

B3143

Puddletown Forest

Icen Way

Acland Rd

A35(T)

Hardy's Cottage

South Walks Rd.

Higher Bockhampton

DORCHESTER

B3150

0   1   2 miles

START/FINISH

112

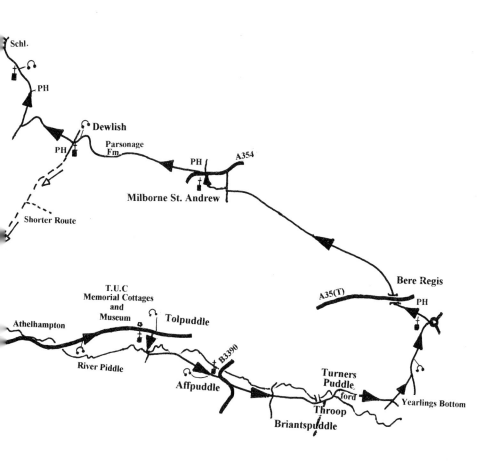

Schl.

PH

Dewlish

Parsonage
Fm.

PH

PH

A354

Milborne St. Andrew

Shorter Route

Bere Regis

T.U.C
Memorial Cottages
and
Museum

Tolpuddle

A35(T)

PH

Athelhampton

River Piddle

B3390

Affpuddle

Turners
Puddle

ford

Throop

Briantspuddle

Yearlings Bottom

Points of interest

▲ Higher Bockhampton: a tiny hamlet with an old thatched cottage, the birthplace of Thomas Hardy and now a National Trust property, on the edge of Puddletown Heath (the 'Egdon Heath' of Hardy's *The Return of the Native*). He also wrote *Under the Greenwood Tree* and *Far from the Madding Crowd* here. His heart is buried with his first wife in the churchyard at Stinsford near by.

▲ Athelhampton: the village contains a fine manor house, mainly fifteenth century with a Tudor great hall and state bedroom and a unique timbered roof. The gardens, designed by Inigo Jones, are a delight; they are open to the public.

▲ Puddletown: an attractive village with a superb fifteenth-century church with box pews, a canopied pulpit and a musicians' gallery which features in Hardy's *Under the Greenwood Tree*. The Norman font is shaped like a medieval wine cup.

▲ Tolpuddle: one of the most famous villages in the world. It became the birthplace of trade unionism when, in 1831, six labourers and the Methodist minister, George Loveless, met together under a large sycamore tree in the village centre to discuss seeking an improvement in wages. Later arrested and transported to Australia for seven years 'as an example', they were eventually pardoned before the end of their term. Opposite the tree there are six cottages, built in 1934 by the TUC, one of which contains the Tolpuddle Martyrs Museum – well worth a visit.

Stage 2: Tolpuddle–Affpuddle–Briantspuddle–Throop–Turners Puddle–Bere Regis

Follow the road and at the fork bear left along the road which passes the entrance to Southover House and runs parallel to the River Piddle. Continue through the village past the church and at the road junction bear right along the B3390 following the signposted direction to Moreton and Crossways. At the next junction leave the B3390 and turn left to Briantspuddle, passing Beehive Cottage on the right.

At the crossroads in Briantspuddle go straight across, towards Throop. The road passes Pipers Cottage at the entrance to the hamlet of Throop. Where the road bears sharp right there is a signpost on the left, indicating a cycle track down to the river. Follow this signposted track across the river to Turners Puddle. At the T-junction turn right and follow the signposted cycle track through Turners Puddle to the T-junction at Yearlings Bottom. Turn left to Bere Regis. The road rises in steps to a junction. Here, bear left to Bere Regis (0.75 miles). Follow the road and turn left near the Royal Oak public house. Ride along West Street, bear right under the A35(T) and follow the road to Milborne St Andrew.

Points of interest

▲ Affpuddle: the village stands on the edge of the heath, Thomas Hardy's 'Great Heath'. The exquisite wood carvings on the bench ends and pulpit in the church are by Thomas Lyllington. A monk and vicar, he came from Cerne Abbas at the Dissolution of the Monasteries, and carved into the woodwork representations of former companions whom he disliked.

▲ Briantspuddle: this attractive village is named after the lord of the manor in the reign of Edward III, Brian Turbeville (the family name behind Hardy's *Tess of the d'Urbervilles*).

▲ Bere Regis: the birthplace of Simon de Montfort, Earl of Leicester (1200–65), founder of the English Parliament. The church is a fifteenth-century building. It has a series of arches supported by columns, known as an arcade, which was built by the Normans. The magnificent timber roof was contributed by John Morton (1420–1500), who was made Archbishop of Canterbury in 1486 and later Lord Chancellor. Members of the Turberville family, relatives of Morton, are buried in the church.

Stage 3: Bere Regis–Milborne St Andrew–Dewlish–Cheselbourne – Piddletrenthide–Piddlehinton

The road from Bere Regis leads to a crossroads on the outskirts of Milborne St Andrew. Go straight across into Milborne St Andrew and follow the road as it descends and bears right to a junction with the A354. Turn left, passing the Royal Oak Inn on the right. At the fork in the road bear right for Dewlish (2 miles) and Cheselbourne (3.5 miles). The route passes Parsonage Farm and crosses Devils Brook before going up through Dewlish to a crossroads. Here there is a choice of routes:

(a) To follow the long route, go straight across and climb to the summit of the hill, from where Cheselbourne can be seen in the valley below. Ride down to a T-junction and turn right for Cheselbourne. Continue through the village past the River Arms Inn and turn left to Piddletrenthide at the junction near the Cheselbourne County School.

The road to Piddletrenthide crosses the undulating chalklands of North Dorset. To the north of Thorncombe Farm can be seen the impressive rim of Lyscombe Hill. The descent to the valley of the River Piddle is steep. Turn left at the junction with the B3143 and follow the road through Piddletrenthide, White Lackington and Piddlehinton. Remain on the B3143 to the junction with the B3150. Turn right, cross Grey's Bridge and return to the car park in Dorchester.

(b) For the shorter route, turn left at the crossroads after Dewlish and follow the road without deviation to a T-junction at Druce Farm. Turn right onto the B3142 and at the junction with the B3143 turn left to Dorchester.

Points of interest

▲ Dewlish: in the nearby chalk hills were found the bones of a pre-Ice Age elephant; these are now in Dorchester's County Museum, along with Bronze Age and Roman artifacts found in the neighbourhood and a tessellated Roman pavement found in the grounds of Dewlish House.

▲ Piddletrenthide: there is a fine Norman church here with fifteenth-century additions and interesting gargoyles.

Ride 24

A TOUR IN AND AROUND MARSHWOOD VALE

Distance: 19 miles **Journey time:** *approximately 5 hours*

Route Description

This tour leaves Lyme Regis and climbs to the perimeter of Marshwood Vale before descending into the village of Monkton Wyld. From here the route takes the rider along quiet lanes, through the forest at Champerhayes Marsh and up to the rim of the vale at Fishpond Bottom and the hill forts of Coney's Castle and Lambert's Castle. At this point and from the church at Marshwood there are wonderful views down into Marshwood Vale and across to Golden Cap on the coast. The ride returns down into the vale and makes its way across to Whitchurch Canonicorum, where it heads towards Charmouth and back to Lyme Regis.

The solitude and charm of Marshwood Vale make it rather special. Hills cannot be avoided in this part of Dorset, but riders are rewarded by the wonderful views along the coast line of Lyme Bay and across the basin-shaped expanse of Marshwood Vale. The main climbs are between Lyme Regis and the summit of Fern Hill, up to Fishpond Bottom and from Charmouth to top of Fern Hill.

Start (OS Landranger sheet 193. Grid reference SY 333918.)

The tour begins from the Pound Street car park in Lyme Regis. From the car park turn right into Pound Street and ride down to and along Broad Street to the traffic lights near the museum. Bear left up Church Street and its continuation, Charmouth Road (the A3052). Turn right at the sign to Timber Hill and continue up the hill past the Lyme Regis Golf Club to the junction with the A3052. This diversion takes you away from the busy Charmouth Road and gives panoramic views over Lyme Regis.

At the summit of Fern Hill, turn right onto the A3052 and take the first turning on the left to Axminster. This leads down a winding road to the A35(T). Turn left onto the A35(T) and take the first turning on the right to Monkton Wyld. Care must be taken when crossing this busy road, particularly during the holiday season.

Points of interest

▲ Lyme Regis: this attractive seaside resort has a fine bay and many charming Georgian buildings; it has long been popular with artists and writers, among them Jane Austen, who set her novel *Persuasion* here. 'Regis' was added to the name in 1284, when Edward I granted the town its first charter. The thirteenth-century Cobb with its twisting stone jetty forms a promenade to shelter the old harbour. It was here that the Duke of

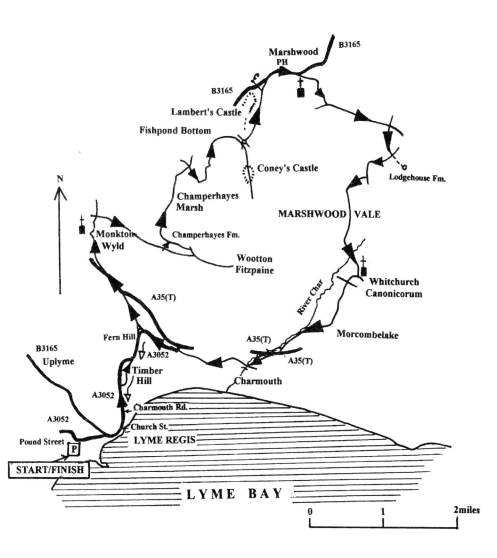

B3165

Marshwood
PH

B3165

Lambert's Castle

Fishpond Bottom

Coney's Castle

Lodgehouse Fm.

Champerhayes
Marsh

MARSHWOOD VALE

N

Champerhayes Fm.

Monkton
Wyld

Wootton
Fitzpaine

River Char

Whitchurch
Canonicorum

A35(T)

Fern Hill

A35(T)

Morcombelake

B3165
Uplyme

A3052

A35(T)

Timber
Hill

A35(T)

A3052

Charmouth

Charmouth Rd.

A3052

Church St.

Pound Street

LYME REGIS

P

START/FINISH

LYME BAY

0   1   2miles

Monmouth landed to gather support for his rebellion against James II. The local museum houses a fine collection of local fossils.

Stage 1: *Monkton Wyld–Fishpond Bottom–Marshwood*

The minor road to Monkton Wyld falls steeply from the A35(T) to the village cross and church. At a signposted crossroads turn right towards Wootton Fitzpaine. The road drops down steeply past Bowshot Farm on the right before rising to a turn on the left to Champernhayes Farm. Turn left and follow the road to a T-junction near the farm. Then turn left again, pass the rear of the farm and continue into the forest at Champernhayes Marsh. Follow the road through the forest, passing a picnic area on the right.

From the picnic area ride on to the next crossroads and turn right to Fishpond Bottom. Continue on this road, pass the church in Fishpond Bottom, and on to a junction of four roads, the centre of which is grassed and signposted. Bear left round the grassed area and take the road diagonally opposite leading to Marshwood; it runs beneath the earthwork fortifications of Lambert's Castle. The entrance to the castle is at this junction.

Follow this road along the rim of Marshwood Vale and at the next junction bear right, passing the Three Counties Nurseries on the left. At the junction with the B3165 (Lyme Regis Road) turn right to Marshwood, passing the Bottle Inn. Take the first turning on the right, signposted to Broad Oak and Mutton Street, at the side of a primary school, bearing left past the Church of St Mary the Virgin. There are magnificent views from behind the church.

Points of interest
▲ Monkton Wyld: a pleasant hamlet on the western side of Marshwood Vale.

Stage 2: *Marshwood–Whitchurch Canonicorum–Charmouth–Lyme Regis*

Continue along the road from the church which leads down into the vale. At the crossroads turn right to Whitchurch and at the next T-junction turn right, passing the entrance to Lodge House Farm on the left. Keep right at the turning to Mandeville Stoke Farm. Cross the River Char and ride to the T-junction at the entrance to Whitchurch Canonicorum. Berehayes Farm is opposite the junction. Turn left to visit the church, and right to continue the journey. Pass the post office and village hall and at the crossroads go straight across. Refreshments can be obtained at Bonhayes Farm on the right.

Follow the road to the junction with the A35(T). Turn right onto the A35(T) and take the first left to Charmouth. Cross the River Char and ride through Charmouth along The Street to the junction with the A3052 and the A35(T). Bear left along the A3052 towards Lyme Regis and climb Fern Hill. From the summit follow the road to Lyme Regis, taking the first turning on the left down Timber Hill. At the T-junction with the A3052 turn left and continue into Lyme Regis and the car park.

Refreshments are readily available in the town and at the restaurant on Marine Parade bicycles can be left safely, within the rider's sight.

Points of interest

▲ Whitchurch Canonicorum: a delightful village, known as 'The Capital of Marshwood'. The fine church contains the shrine of St Wite. This has three holes, into which pilgrims traditionally put their diseased limbs or the clothes of a sick person for healing. In the churchyard is the grave of Sir George Somers, who discovered Bermuda.

▲ Charmouth: a small seaside resort with some Regency buildings, often visited by Jane Austen. Catherine of Aragon stayed at its oldest public house, the Queen's Arms, in 1501 and Prince Charles took refuge there before his flight to France in 1651. In 1811 a twelve-year-old girl, Mary Anning, found a 150-million-year-old fossilized ichthyosaurus in the cliff face. Her later discoveries included the first known plesiosaur and pterodactyl. A number of her discoveries are displayed in the Natural History Museum in London.

Fossil-hunting on the beach, Charmouth

Ride 25

WAREHAM TO SWANAGE ACROSS THE HEATHLAND AND THE PURBECK HILLS

Distance: 25 miles Journey time: approximately 6 hours

Route Description

The tour starts in Wareham and crosses heathland, which provides a perfect foreground for the first view of Corfe Castle. At this village, set in a gap in the Purbeck Hills, the ride joins a minor road to Swanage. From this undulating but little-used road there are excellent views across the valley to the coastal ridge. The first view of the sea and coastline followed by the long downhill run into Swanage are further high points.

The return route from Swanage is via the coastal ridge and involves a gradual climb to a point just beyond Langton Matravers, where the road levels out. The journey to Worth Matravers is rewarded by sea views, strip lynchets and ancient field patterns along the cliff tops. The village churchyard contains the grave of Benjamin Jesty, who achieved fame as a pioneer in vaccination against smallpox.

The ride returns to Corfe Castle via Kingston and climbs to the ridge of the Purbeck Hills above Cocknowle. From there the final stage is to Stoborough Green and Wareham.

This route is best suited to the regular rider as there are quite a number of hills to be climbed. However, alternative and less strenuous routes can be taken by using the train from Corfe Castle to Swanage.

Start (OS Landranger 195. Grid reference SY 920872.)

From the car park in Strechie Road, Wareham, turn left into West Street and at the crossroads turn right into South Street. Follow the road past The Quay, cross the bridge over the River Frome and continue along the B3075. Take the first left (Nutcrack Lane) after the King's Arms public house.

Points of interest

▲ Wareham: site of an Anglo-Saxon town and port with an Anglo-Saxon street plan and the remains of ramparts on three sides of the town. In St Martin's Church, which dates from 1030, there is a marble effigy of T.E. Lawrence lying in his desert robes, and the parish church of Lady St Mary (rebuilt in 1842) contains many relics and features of interest. The quay area declined in importance in the eighteenth century but is still worth seeing.

Stage 1: Wareham–Corfe Castle–Swanage

Follow the road and ride straight ahead at the crossroads. Pass Old Kiln Road on the left,

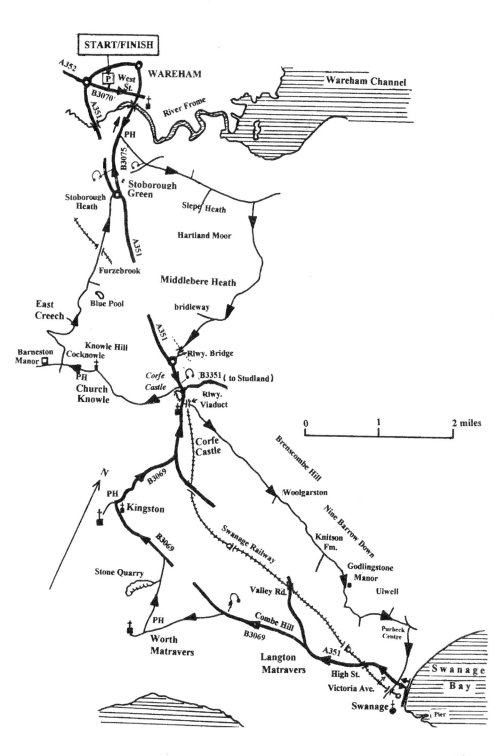

START/FINISH

A352

WAREHAM

P West St.

B3070

A351

B3075

Wareham Channel

River Frome

PH

Stoborough Green

Stoborough Heath

Slepe Heath

Hartland Moor

A351

Furzebrook

Middlebere Heath

East Creech

Blue Pool

bridleway

Knowle Hill
Cocknowle

A351

Barneston Manor

Rlwy. Bridge

PH

Corfe Castle

B3351 (to Studland)

Church Knowle

Rlwy. Viaduct

0   1   2 miles

Corfe Castle

Brenscombe Hill

B3069

PH

Kingston

Woolgarston

Swanage Railway

Nine Barrow Down

B3069

Knitson Fm.

N

Stone Quarry

Godlingstone Manor

Valley Rd.

Ulwell

PH

Worth Matravers

Combe Hill

B3069

Purbeck Centre

Langton Matravers

A351

Swanage Bay

High St.

Victoria Ave.

Swanage

Pier

ignore the grated turning on the right and take the signposted right turn to Corfe Castle. The road crosses Hartland Moor and Middlebere Heath. The first sight of the castle occurs near Maranoa Farm.

Continue straight on past the bridleway to Norden, cross the old railway bridge and ride to the T-junction. Turn right for access to the roundabout and join the A351 (left) to Corfe Castle. Disregarding the road to Studland on the left, ride up East Street, alongside the castle mound, and take the first left turn up Sandy Lane. This lane is just short of the Greyhound Inn, between two houses. Pass under the railway bridge and follow this narrow road as it runs beneath Brenscombe Hill, passing Woolgarston, Knitson Farm and Godlingston Manor Farm. Keep straight on to Ulwell, ignoring the wide turning to the right just beyond Godlingston Manor.

At the T-junction in Ulwell turn right and then right again at the roundabout down Northbrook Road. Go past the Purbeck Centre to the junction with Victoria Avenue. Turn left, go straight across at the traffic lights and ride to Swanage sea front. The centre of the town can be reached by walking or riding along Shore Road.

Points of interest
▲   Corfe Castle: a lovely village overlooked by the castle ruins. The castle was built by the Normans on the site of a Saxon hunting lodge and stands in a cleft in the Purbeck

Corfe Castle

Hills. Edward the Martyr was murdered there in 978. During the Civil War Lady Bankes successfully defended the castle against Cromwell's forces, but she was then betrayed and Parliament ordered it to be destroyed.

▲ Swanage: a former Anglo-Saxon port where King Alfred defeated the Danish fleet in 877. The town hall has an elaborate Wren façade brought from London. The town is a popular holiday resort, the Swanage Railway providing a rail service to Corfe Castle.

Stage 2: Swanage–Langton Matravers–Worth Matravers–Kingston–Corfe Castle

The return journey from Swanage starts from Victoria Avenue and follows the A351 across the Swanage railway bridge to the junction with the B3069. Bear left to Langton Matravers. The gradual climb from Swanage continues through the village to the Worth Matravers junction, where the road becomes reasonably level.

Turn left to Worth Matravers. On the journey to the village there are fine sea views and clearly identifiable strip lynchets and outlines of ancient field boundaries in the fields along the cliff tops. The church lies beyond the Square and Compass Inn.

Turn right by the inn and return to the B3069, passing a quarry on the left. Turn left at the junction with the B3069. There are excellent views of Corfe Castle at this point. From here the road leads to Kingston, turning sharp right at the Scott Arms, from where it descends steeply to the A351. Turn left at the junction with the A351 and ride through Corfe Castle, past the Bankes Arms and the Greyhound Inn, and take the first turning on the left.

Points of interest

▲ Worth Matravers: a small village surrounded by evidence of early man's habitation. The mainly Norman church is constructed from locally quarried stone. Benjamin Jesty (1736–1816), who pioneered vaccination against smallpox, is buried with his wife in the churchyard.

▲ Kingston: the village commands a wonderful view of Corfe Castle. In 1880 the Third Lord Eldon thought the original church too small and built a second one, which is referred to as 'The Cathedral of the Downs'.

Stage 3: Corfe Castle–Church Knowle–Furzebrook–Stoborough–Wareham

This road bears left around the castle mound, crosses a river bridge and heads towards Church Knowle. Pass through Church Knowle and at the crossroads turn right towards Stoborough. The road rises up through Cocknowle to a viewing point on the ridge of the Purbeck Hills. From here the road descends steeply to a very sharp right-hand bend, then runs alongside an exposed limestone quarry face.

Carry straight on at the junction to East Creech and head towards Furzebrook. A visit to the Blue Pool can be made on this section of the journey. Pass through Furzebrook and continue to the roundabout on the A351. Turn left and take the second exit to Stoborough Green. Great care has to be taken on this busy roundabout. Enter Wareham along South Street (the B3075), turn left at the traffic lights and return to the car park on West Street.

Points of interest

▲ The Blue Pool: between Church Knowle and Furzebrook, once a clay pit but now a beautiful blue lake.

Alternative routes:

(a) Cycle from Wareham to Corfe Castle using the route guide for Stage 1. Travel by steam train from Corfe Castle to Swanage with a return ticket (bicycles are carried free of charge). Return to Corfe Castle and cycle to Wareham via Church Knowle, Furzebrook and Stoborough using the route guide for Stage 3 or return across the heathland.

(b) Cycle from Wareham to Corfe Castle using the route guide for Stage 1. Travel by steam train to Swanage with a single ticket (bicycles are carried free of charge). Cycle back to Wareham via Langton Matravers, Worth Matravers, Kingston and Corfe Castle using the route guide for Stage 2. From Corfe Castle, you can return to Wareham across the heathland, using the route guide for Stage 1, or via Church Knowle, Furzebrook and Stoborough, using the route guide for Stage 3.

Bicycle Shops, Repair and Hire

Blandford Forum	Lucas Cycles 38 Salisbury Street	(01258) 452532
Bridport	Wheels and Deals (Hire) 37 St Michaels Trading Estate	(01308) 420586
Bournemouth	Rayboulds Raleigh Centre 579-581 Wimborne Road	(01202) 529061
Bournemouth	On Yer Bike (Hire) 88 Charminster Road	(01202) 315855
Dorchester	Dorchester Cycles 316 Great Western Road	(01305) 268787
Dorchester	Auto-Bitz 48 High East Street	(01305) 262095
Gillingham	Wheels Cycles Station Road	(01747) 825757
Poole	B.J. Cycles (Hire) 196 Blandford Road Hamworthy, Poole	(01202) 671148
Sherborne	Brian Hoppé Cycles Trendle Street	(01935) 812038
Sherborne	Automotive 24 Cheap Street	(01935) 812289
Stalbridge	Dorset Cycles (Hire) 31 High Street	(01963) 362476
Sturminster Marshall	Paul's Cycle Service Unit 3 Bailey Gate Industrial Estate	(01258) 857165
Swanage	Purbeck Pedal Power Court Road	(01929) 426631

Wareham	Wareham Sports and Cycles 28 South Street	(01929) 552774
Weymouth	Westham Cycles 128 Abbotsbury Road	(01305) 776977
Weymouth	Samways (G.M. & D.A. Cribb) 14 Crescent Street	(01305) 776977
Wimborne	Samways & Son 70 Leigh Road	(01202) 882960

Tourist Information Centres

Blandford	West Street	(01258) 454770
Bournemouth	Westover Road	(01202) 789789
Bridport	32 South Street	(01308) 424901
Christchurch	23 High Street	(01202) 471780
Dorchester	1 Acland Road	(01305) 267992
Lyme Regis	Guildhall Cottage	(01297) 442138
Lyndhurst (including the New Forest)	The Centre Car Park, High Street	(01703) 282269
Mere	The Square	(01747) 860341
Poole	36 Priory Quay, Christchurch	(01202) 673322
Shaftesbury	Bell Street	(01747) 853514
Sherborne	3 Tilton Court, Digby Road	(01935) 815341
Swanage	The White House, Shore Road	(01929) 432885
Wareham	East Street	(01929) 552740
Weymouth	The Esplanade	(01305) 785747
Wimborne	29 High Street	(01202) 886116

Notes